DEFINING MOMENTS
THE INTERNET REVOLUTION

DEFINING MOMENTS
THE INTERNET REVOLUTION

Kevin Hillstrom

Omnigraphics

615 Griswold, Detroit MI 48226

Omnigraphics, Inc.

Kevin Hillstrom, *Series Editor*
Cherie D. Abbey, *Managing Editor*

Peter E. Ruffner, *Publisher*
Frederick G. Ruffner, Jr., *Chairman*
Matthew P. Barbour, *Senior Vice President*

Kay Gill, *Vice President – Directories*
Elizabeth Barbour, *Research and Permissions Coordinator*
David P. Bianco, *Marketing Director*
Leif Gruenberg, *Development Manager*
Kevin Hayes, *Operations Manager*

Barry Puckett, *Librarian*
Cherry Stockdale, *Permissions Assistant*
Shirley Amore, Don Brown, John L. Chetcuti, Kevin Glover, Martha Johns, Kirk Kauffman, *Administrative Staff*

Library of Congress Cataloging-in-Publication Data

Hillstrom, Kevin, 1963-
    Defining moments : the Internet revolution / Kevin Hillstrom.
       p. cm.
    Includes bibliographical references and index.
    ISBN 0-7808-0767-7 (hardcover : alk. paper)
    [1. Internet--History.] I. Title.
    TK5105.875.I57H54 2005
    004.67'8'09--dc22

                  2005007303

TABLE OF CONTENTS

PRIMARY SOURCES

PREFACE

Throughout the course of America's existence, its people, culture, and institutions have been periodically challenged—and in many cases transformed— by profound historical events. Some of these momentous events, such as women's suffrage, the civil rights movement, and U.S. involvement in World War II, invigorated the nation and strengthened American confidence and capabilities. Others, such as the McCarthy era, the Vietnam War, and Watergate, have prompted troubled assessments and heated debates about the country's core beliefs and character.

Some of these defining moments in American history were years or even decades in the making. The Harlem Renaissance and the New Deal, for example, unfurled over the span of several years, while the American labor movement and the Cold War evolved over the course of decades. Other defining moments, such as the Cuban missile crisis and the terrorist attacks of September 11, 2001, transpired over a matter of days or weeks.

But although significant differences exist among these events in terms of their duration and their place in the timeline of American history, all share the same basic characteristic: they transformed the United States' political, cultural, and social landscape for future generations of Americans.

Taking heed of this fundamental reality, American citizens, schools, and other institutions are increasingly emphasizing the importance of understanding our nation's history. Omnigraphics' new *Defining Moments* series was created for the express purpose of meeting this growing appetite for authoritative, useful historical resources. This new series, which focuses on the most pivotal events in U.S. history from the 20th century forward, will be of enduring value to anyone interested in learning more about America's past—and in understanding how those historical events continue to reverberate in the 21st century.

Each individual volume of *Defining Moments* provides a valuable resource for readers interested in learning about the most profound events in our nation's history. Each volume is organized into three distinct sections— Narrative Overview, Biographies, and Primary Sources.

- The **Narrative Overview** provides readers with a detailed, factual account of the origins and progression of the "defining moment" being examined. It also explores the event's lasting impact on America's political and cultural landscape.

- The **Biographies** section provides valuable biographical background on leading figures associated with the event in question. Each biography concludes with a list of sources for further information on the profiled individual.

- The **Primary Sources** section collects a wide variety of pertinent primary source materials from the era under discussion, including official documents, papers and resolutions, letters, oral histories, memoirs, editorials, and other important works.

Individually, each of these sections is a rich resource for users. Together, they comprise an authoritative, balanced, and absorbing examination of some of the most significant events in U.S. history.

Other notable features contained within each volume in the series include a glossary of important individuals, places, and terms; a detailed chronology featuring page references to relevant sections of the narrative; an annotated bibliography of sources for further study; an extensive general bibliography that reflects the wide range of historical sources consulted by the author; and a subject index.

Acknowledgements

This series was developed in consultation with a distinguished Advisory Board comprised of public librarians, school librarians, and educators. They evaluated the series as it developed, and their comments and suggestions were invaluable throughout the production process. Any errors in this and other volumes in the series are ours alone. Following is a list of board members who contributed to the *Defining Moments* series:

Gail Beaver, M.A., M.A.L.S.
\Adjunct Lecturer, University of Michigan
Ann Arbor, MI

Melissa C. Bergin, L.M.S., NBCT
Niskayuna High School
Niskayuna, NY

Rose Davenport, M.S.L.S., Ed.Specialist
Library Media Specialist
Pershing High School Library
Detroit, MI

Karen Imarisio, A.M.L.S.
Assistant Head of Adult Services
Bloomfield Twp. Public Library
Bloomfield Hills, MI

Nancy Larsen, M.L.S., M.S. Ed.
Library Media Specialist
Clarkston High School
Clarkston, MI

Marilyn Mast, M.I.L.S.
Kingswood Campus Librarian
Cranbrook Kingswood Upper School
Bloomfield Hills, MI

Rosemary Orlando, M.L.I.S.
Assistant Director
St. Clair Shores Public Library
St. Clair Shores, MI

Comments and Suggestions

We welcome your comments on *Defining Moments: The Internet Revolution* and suggestions for other events in U.S. history that warrant treatment in the *Defining Moments* series. Correspondence should be addressed to:

Editor, *Defining Moments*
Omnigraphics, Inc.
615 Griswold
Detroit, MI 48226
E-mail: editorial@omnigraphics.com

HOW TO USE THIS BOOK

Defining Moments: The Internet Revolution provides users with a detailed and authoritative overview of the era, as well as the principal figures involved in this pivotal event in U.S. history. The preparation and arrangement of this volume—and all other books in the *Defining Moments* series—reflect an emphasis on providing a thorough and objective account of events that shaped our nation, presented in an easy-to-use reference work.

Defining Moments: The Internet Revolution is divided into three primary sections. The first of these sections, **Narrative Overview**, provides a detailed, factual account of the origin and development of the Internet Revolution. It explores the early days of the Internet and the World Wide Web, tracks the peaks and valleys of the "dot.com" explosion of the 1990s, discusses the promise and peril of the modern Internet, and examines the potential impact of the Internet in years to come, both in the United States and around the world.

The second section, **Biographies**, provides valuable biographical background on leading figures involved in the creation and growth of the Internet, including Vinton Cerf, a pioneer in Internet architecture; Tim Berners-Lee, inventor of the World Wide Web; and Sergey Brin and Larry Page, creators of the Google Internet search engine. Each biography concludes with a list of sources for further information on the profiled individual.

The third section, **Primary Sources**, gathers fascinating documents that illuminate the early history of the Internet and its impact on commerce and culture around the world. Documents include the first World Wide Web page to feature hypertext links; John Perry Barlow's "Declaration of Independence for Cyberspace"; and Bill Gates's forward-looking "Generation I" speech at the New York Institute of Technology. Other primary sources featured in

Defining Moments: The Internet Revolution include excerpts from official documents, papers, essays, speeches, and other important works.

Other valuable features in *Defining Moments: The Internet Revolution* include the following:

- Attribution and referencing of primary sources and other quoted material to help guide users to other valuable historical research resources.
- Glossary of Important People, Places, and Terms.
- Detailed Chronology of events with a *see reference* feature. Under this arrangement, events listed in the chronology include a reference to page numbers within the Narrative Overview wherein users can find additional information on the event in question.
- Photographs of the leading figures and major events of the Internet Revolution.
- Sources for Further Study, an annotated list of noteworthy Internet-related works.
- Extensive bibliography of works consulted in the creation of this book, including books, periodicals, Internet sites, and videotape materials.
- A Subject Index.

IMPORTANT PEOPLE, PLACES, AND TERMS

Advanced Research Projects Agency (ARPA)
Agency formed by the U.S. Department of Defense in 1957 to develop new technology for military and scientific use

Andreessen, Marc
Co-inventor of Mosaic, one of the first successful Web browsers, and founder of Netscape Communications

ARPANET
The world's first computer network, developed by Advanced Research Projects Agency (ARPA) researchers in 1969, and a precursor to the modern Internet

Barlow, John Perry
Writer, legal expert, and co-founder of the Electronic Frontier Foundation, and a leading proponent of free speech on and open access to the Internet

Berners-Lee, Tim
Computer expert and inventor of the World Wide Web

Bolt Beranek and Newman (BBN)
Technology consulting firm based in Boston, Massachusetts, that built the first Interface Message Processors (IMPs) for the ARPANET

Brin, Sergey
Co-inventor of Google, the first Internet search engine to rank Web sites based on the number of links they receive from other sites

Broadband
Various types of Internet connections—including Digital Subscriber Lines (DSL), cable modems, and Wi-Fi—that offer greater bandwidth and faster download speeds than traditional dial-up telephone access

Browser
> *See* Web browser

Case, Steve
> Co-founder of America Online (AOL), the most popular Internet Service Provider (ISP) in the United States

Cerf, Vinton
> Computer scientist often referred to as "Father of the Internet" for his role in testing the original Interface Message Processors (IMPs), developing the TCP/IP protocols, and leading the first test of the Internet

Crocker, Stephen
> Computer researcher who wrote the first Request for Comments (RFC), thus launching a process of collaborative decision making that continues to guide the development of the Internet

Defense Advanced Research Projects Agency (DARPA)
> *See* Advanced Research Projects Agency (ARPA)

Digital divide
> The idea that Internet access tends to vary among certain socioeconomic groups, creating a division between "haves" and "have nots"

Domain Name System (DNS)
> A hierarchical structure for the names of Internet host computers that begins with the most specific identifier and ends with a general classification or domain

Dot.com
> Shorthand term for Internet businesses, taken from the three-letter domain abbreviation for commercial Web sites (.com)

Electronic commerce (e-commerce)
> Doing business over the Internet or on the World Wide Web

Electronic mail (e-mail)
> An Internet-based communications program that allows users to exchange messages and information

Filo, David
> Co-founder of Yahoo!, the popular search engine and Web portal

Gates, Bill
> Founder of Microsoft, the world's most influential maker of computer operating systems and software applications

Gopher
> One of the earliest software programs intended to help users locate information on the Internet, created at the University of Minnesota in the 1980s

Gore, Al
> Former U.S. Senator from Tennessee and Vice President of the United States who emerged as an early champion for expanding public and commercial use of the Internet

Graphical User Interface (GUI)
> A program that allows users to interact with their computers through a visual display, primarily using a pointing device (like a computer mouse) rather than typing commands on a keyboard

Hacker
> A person who uses computer expertise to break into software programs and computer systems, usually to steal or damage data

Hypertext
> A technological concept which provided a method for creating electronic links between text documents

Hypertext Markup Language (HTML)
> A coding system that uses embedded commands or tags to identify the various elements in a document, but lets individual computers decide how to display these elements

Hypertext Transfer Protocol (HTTP)
> A set of rules or instructions that enables different Internet servers to communicate and share information

Hyperlink
> An embedded HTML code that appears on the computer screen as a highlighted word or image and allows users to jump instantly to related information with a click of the mouse

Information Processing Techniques Office (IPTO)
The division of the Advanced Projects Research Agency (ARPA) that conducted research into computer networking, leading to creation of the ARPANET

Interface Message Processor (IMP)
Refrigerator-sized minicomputers that translated information flowing between supercomputers connected to the ARPANET

Internet
A vast global network of interconnected computer networks

Internet Protocol
See Transmission Control Protocol/Internet Protocol (TCP/IP)

Internet Relay Chat (IRC)
A protocol that allows users to converse with others in real time

Internet Service Provider (ISP)
Any enterprise that offers Internet access to groups of users

Kahn, Robert
Computer scientist who gave the first public demonstration of the ARPANET and helped develop the TCP/IP protocol

Kleinrock, Leonard
Computer scientist who wrote the first academic paper describing packet-switching theory and oversaw installation of the first node of the ARPANET at UCLA

Licklider, J.C.R.
Computer scientist who first described the process of linking computers into a "Galactic Network"; director of the Information Processing Techniques Office (IPTO)

Local Area Network (LAN)
A computer network that connect computers in a relatively small area, such as an office

Mosaic
One of the earliest Web browsers, developed by Marc Andreessen and colleagues at the University of Illinois and later commercialized as Netscape Navigator

NSFnet
A research-oriented computer network operated by the National Science Foundation that was a precursor to the modern Internet

Node
On a computer network, an intersection that features a device capable of processing or forwarding data transmissions

Open-architecture networking
A key technical idea that allowed different types of networks to be connected together through the Internet, using a shared network protocol to define how they communicated with each other

Packet switching
Method used to transmit data over the Internet; entails breaking information into small units called packets, sending the packets toward their destination on any available connection, and reassembling the packets once they arrive

Page, Larry
Co-inventor of Google, the first Internet search engine to rank Web sites based on the number of links they receive from other sites

Polly, Jean Armour
A librarian and writer who coined the term "surfing" to describe the process of exploring the World Wide Web and searching for information on the Internet

Postel, Jonathan
Computer scientist who helped guide the collaborative development of the Internet as longtime editor of the "Request for Comments" (RFC) series

Protocol
A fundamental rule or principle guiding the operation of a computer network, such as the Internet (*see also* Transmission Control Protocol/Internet Protocol)

Radio-Frequency Identification (RFID)
A system of electronic sensors that can be attached to objects, providing constant wireless transmissions regarding the objects' location and status

Request for Comments (RFC)
> A series of thousands of memos that document the technical development of the Internet

Roberts, Larry
> Computer scientist who decided to adopt packet-switching as the basis of the ARPANET and became a leading proponent of collaborative development and information sharing

Router
> A powerful computer that reads the "address" inside packets of information and decides how best to send each packet toward its final destination over the Internet

Search engine
> Sophisticated programs that help users locate information on the Internet by comparing search terms to a database containing subject and keyword information for millions of Web pages, and returning a list of documents containing those terms

Spam
> Unsolicited junk e-mail messages sent out in mass mailings by commercial enterprises

Spyware
> A hidden software program that tracks which Web sites a user visits and uses the information to deliver self-launching advertisements (pop-up ads) targeted specifically toward the user's interests

Taylor, Robert
> Director of the Information Processing Techniques Office (IPTO) who oversaw development of the ARPANET in the 1960s

Transmission Control Protocol/Internet Protocol (TCP/IP)
> A set of rules guiding the operation of all computers connected to the Internet; TCP is responsible for breaking down information into packets and then reassembling the packets in the proper order, while IP controls the process of addressing packets so that routers know where to send them

Tomlinson, Ray
> A computer engineer at Bolt Beranek and Newman (BBN) who developed the first modern electronic mail (e-mail) program

Uniform Resource Locator (URL)

A textual address created using the Domain Name System (DNS) that identifies the unique location of a Web page on the Internet, allowing connected computers to find and retrieve it

Virus

A malicious software program designed to destroy data and disable computer systems

Voice-over-Internet Protocol (VoIP)

A technology that breaks voice transmissions into packets of data that can be sent over the Internet

Web browser

A software program that retrieves pages from Web servers, interprets the Hypertext Markup Language (HTML) codes embedded within them, and display the information on a computer screen

Web site

A collection of related documents or pages on the World Wide Web that are connected to each other using hypertext links

Wireless networking

A network in which there are no physical connections between computers; instead, the computers communicate using radio-frequency signals

Wi-Fi

Short for wireless-fidelity networking, an emerging technology that allows computers to connect to the Internet remotely

Wi-Max

A future generation of wireless-fidelity networking (Wi-Fi) that is predicted to give wireless connectivity the capacity to cover entire cities rather than small local areas

World Wide Web

A sophisticated combination of software programs and networking protocols that run on the Internet

Worm

A malicious software program that spreads from computer to computer across a network, overwhelming systems with mail or unnecessary tasks and often causing them to crash

Yang, Jerry

Co-founder of Yahoo!, the popular search engine and Web portal

CHRONOLOGY

1957

The Soviet Union launches *Sputnik,* the world's first artificial satellite, into orbit. *See p. 6.*

1958

U.S. President Dwight Eisenhower creates the Advanced Research Projects Agency (ARPA) within the Department of Defense. *See p. 6.*

1961

Leonard Kleinrock, a computer science expert at the University of California-Los Angeles (UCLA), publishes the first paper on packet-switching theory. *See p. 9.*

Researchers Paul Baran at the Rand Corporation and Donald Davies at the National Physical Laboratory in England develop packet-switching theory independently of Kleinrock. *See p. 9.*

1962

J.C.R. Licklider becomes director of ARPA's Information Processing Techniques Office (IPTO). *See p. 6.*

Licklider publishes an academic paper describing his vision of a "Galactic Network" of interconnected computers that would allow people to access information from any site around the world. *See p. 6.*

1966

Bob Taylor becomes director of IPTO and launches the ARPANET project. *See p. 7.*

1968

ARPA managers hire Bolt Beranek and Newman (BBN), a small consulting firm based in Cambridge, Massachusetts, to develop key components of the ARPANET. *See p. 10.*

1969

BBN engineers deliver the first Interface Message Processor (IMP) to Leonard Kleinrock at UCLA. *See p. 11.*

Some of Kleinrock's graduate students—including Vinton Cerf, Steve Crocker, and Jonathan Postel—write the software program that connects UCLA's mainframe to the IMP. *See p. 11.*

Kleinrock supervises the initial test of computer-to-computer communication over the ARPANET. *See p. 11.*

The ARPANET is formally commissioned; it originally consists of four nodes. *See p. 11.*

Bob Taylor leaves ARPA and is replaced by Larry Roberts. *See p. 12.*

Crocker seeks input from other researchers by issuing the first Request for Comments (RFC1). *See p. 13.*

1971

The ARPANET expands to include 15 additional nodes, including one at the National Aeronautics and Space Administration (NASA). *See p. 12.*

BBN researcher Ray Tomlinson invents the first modern electronic mail program. *See p. 16.*

1972

Bob Kahn of BBN gives the first public demonstration of the ARPANET at the International Conference on Computer Communications in Washington, D.C. *See p. 17.*

Kahn leaves BBN to take a job with ARPA, eventually replacing Roberts as director of IPTO. *See p. 17.*

1973

Kahn and Cerf outline their plan for "open-architecture networking," a method by which different types of networks can be connected together through the Internet. *See p. 18.*

The first international hosts are connected to the ARPANET. *See p. 18.*

1974

Kahn and Cerf publish an academic paper called "A Protocol for Packet Network Intercommunication" in May 1974. The paper details a set of network communication rules collectively known as Transmission Control Protocol (TCP). *See p. 18.*

1975

Bill Gates founds Microsoft. *See p. 15.*

1977

Vint Cerf conducts an elaborate test that demonstrates the possibilities of interconnected networks, or "internetworking." *See p. 18.*

1978

Cerf and Kahn split their protocol into two parts, TCP and IP (internetwork protocol), to make it less complicated and reduce the demands on gateways and individual networks. *See p. 19.*

1979

The National Science Foundation creates NSFnet, a research-oriented sister network to the ARPANET, with the goal of spreading supercomputer access to researchers at all universities in the United States through internetworking technology. *See p. 20.*

1981

IBM introduces its personal computer (PC).

1982

The number of nodes on the ARPANET reaches 200. *See p. 20.*

The computer mouse first becomes commercially available.

1983

The ARPANET completes the transition to TCP/IP. *See p. 20.*

The NSFnet is linked to the ARPANET. *See p. 20.*

Desktop PC workstations are introduced and Local Area Networks (LANs) begin to form.

1984

The Domain Name System (DNS) comes into use. *See p. 26.*

The number of nodes on the ARPANET surpasses 1,000.

1985

The number of nodes on the ARPANET exceeds 2,000.

1987

The number of nodes on the ARPANET surpasses 10,000.

1988

The first computer virus, known as the Internet Worm of 1988, is released on the Internet on November 1. It disables about 6,000 host computers and calls attention to security concerns on the network. *See p. 21.*

Internet Relay Chat (IRC) is invented.

1989

Tim Berners-Lee invents the combination of software programs and networking protocols known as the World Wide Web. *See p. 24.*

The number of nodes on the ARPANET breaks 100,000.

1990

An early version of the World Wide Web is unrolled for testing. *See p. 26.*

The ARPANET is officially decommissioned and NSFnet becomes the foundation of the Internet. *See p. 22.*

1991

Two students from the University of Minnesota release Gopher, a program that makes it easier to locate information on the Internet. *See p. 23.*

The World Wide Web is made available to the public for the first time. *See p. 26.*

The High-Performance Computing Act of 1991 is passed, authorizing the creation of the National Research and Education Network (NREN) under the NSF. *See p. 47.*

1992

The National Science Foundation issues an "acceptable use policy" that expands the NSFnet's purpose beyond research and development, thus opening the Internet for commercial use. *See p. 46.*

The Information Infrastructure and Technology Act of 1992 is passed, transferring responsibility for the operation of NREN from the NSF to telecommunications companies and other private interests. *See p. 47.*

The number of hosts on the Internet surpasses 1 million.

1993

The number of hosts on the Internet breaks 2 million, and total of Internet users reaches an estimated 3 million worldwide.

Marc Andreessen and colleagues at the University of Illinois release Mosaic, one of the first Web browsers offering a graphical user interface, in March 1993. *See p. 28.*

The White House opens its first Web site. *See p. 30.*

1994

Andreessen leaves college and founds Netscape Communications to commercialize the Mosaic browser. *See p. 29.*

The Internet connects an estimated 38 million people worldwide.

There are approximately 10,000 sites on the World Wide Web.

The Internet Service Provider (ISP) America Online (AOL) boasts one million members. *See p. 31.*

1995

The NSFnet reverts back to a research-oriented network, leaving interconnected private ISPs to provide the backbone of the Internet. *See p. 48.*

Sun Microsystems introduces the Java programming language, which allows Web site designers to incorporate animation and make their sites interactive. *See p. 49.*

Jerry Yang and David Filo form Yahoo! to market their Internet search engine. *See p. 49.*

Jeff Bezos launches the online bookstore Amazon.com. *See p. 50.*

The electronic auction site eBay comes online. *See p. 50.*

Microsoft develops the Internet Explorer browser to compete with Netscape Navigator, and chooses to integrate the program with its popular Windows operating system, thus launching the "browser wars." *See p. 52.*

Netscape holds a historic initial public stock offering on August 8 that is largely credited with giving rise to the rush of Internet start-up businesses known as the "dot.com" boom. *See p. 53.*

1996

The number of Internet users worldwide is estimated at 45 million.

There are approximately 650,000 sites on the World Wide Web.

Responding to passage of the Communications Decency Act by the U.S. Congress, John Perry Barlow publishes his influential essay "A Declaration of Independence for Cyberspace." *See p. 85.*

1997

The U.S. Justice Department files an antitrust lawsuit against Microsoft on behalf of Netscape and other competitors, charging that Microsoft engaged in monopolistic practices in order to drive these companies out of business. *See p. 55.*

1998

Sergey Brin and Larry Page form a company, Google Inc., to promote their revolutionary new search engine.

1999

The number of Internet users worldwide grows to 150 million.

College student Shawn Fanning introduces the file-sharing software Napster, which encourages millions of users to begin illegally downloading digital songs. *See p. 50.*

Netscape Communications loses the browser wars and is acquired by America Online (AOL). *See p. 55.*

The U.S. Department of Commerce issues its famous study called *Falling Through the Net: Defining the Digital Divide. See p. 70.*

The Melissa virus, which is the first to automatically send copies of itself to everyone on an infected computer's e-mail address list, is released and causes $80 million in damage. *See p. 83.*

The Internet2 project comes online, providing a forum for advanced networking experiments. *See p. 90.*

2000

The number of Internet users worldwide reaches 300 million.

Microsoft is found in violation of U.S. antitrust laws in June and is ordered to break into two separate businesses. *See p. 55.*

A dozen fledgling Internet companies spend $2 million each for 30-second commercial spots during the Super Bowl telecast in January. *See p. 59.*

Yahoo!'s stock price reaches $250 per share, giving the company $133 billion in market capital. *See p. 58.*

AOL purchases the media conglomerate Time Warner.

The tech-heavy NASDAQ stock exchange closes at an all-time high of 5,048.62 points on March 13. *See p. 58.*

Acting on news that Microsoft has failed to settle its antitrust lawsuit, investors begin bailing out of the stock market and the "dot.com bubble" begins to burst. On April

4 the Dow Jones Industrial Average declines by 349.15 points–the biggest one-day point drop in its history–losing 7.64 percent of its value. *See p. 61.*

Google officially becomes the world's largest search engine with its introduction of a billion-page index.

Internet voting is first used in the United States during the Arizona Democratic primary, when half of all voters cast their ballots online. *See p. 74.*

2001

The number of sites on the World Wide Web is estimated at 30 million.

Microsoft announces that it has reached a deal with the Justice Department to settle the antitrust case. The deal enables the company to avoid splitting into separate businesses. *See p. 56.*

2002

Napster loses a copyright infringement lawsuit brought by the Recording Industry Association of America and is forced to shut down. *See p. 85.*

2003

Unsolicited junk messages known as "spam" account for over one-half of all e-mail sent. The U.S. Congress responds by passing legislation aimed at stopping spam, including the CAN-SPAM (Controlling the Assault of Non-Solicited Pornography and Marketing) Act of 2003. *See p. 81.*

Consumer spending on the Internet approaches $100 billion.

Despite the shutdown of Napster, Internet users continue to download 2.6 billion music files illegally every month. *See p. 85.*

2004

The number of Internet users worldwide is estimated at 800 million, including 207 million in the United States.

The number of sites on the World Wide Web is estimated at 4.2 billion.

Vermont Governor Howard Dean demonstrates the value of the Internet for fundraising during his bid for the 2004 Democratic presidential nomination. Other candidates quickly adopt the Internet as well, and online political spending reaches $25 million. *See p. 74.*

Google holds a successful initial public stock offering on August 19, raising the possibility of a new wave of Internet investment.

NARRATIVE OVERVIEW

PROLOGUE

In February 1966 Bob Taylor found himself growing increasingly frustrated with what he called his "terminal problem." At the time, Taylor was the director of the Information Processing Techniques Office (IPTO), a computer research division of the Advanced Research Projects Agency (ARPA) at the U.S. Department of Defense. The targets of Taylor's anger were three computer terminals scattered across his Pentagon office. Each of these terminals connected with a different research institution that was working on a computer technology project for IPTO. One terminal connected to the Massachusetts Institute of Technology (MIT), the second to the University of California at Berkeley, and the third to the Systems Development Corporation in California.

With each passing morning, Taylor became progressively more annoyed at the necessity of logging into three different computer terminals in order to track the progress of his researchers. "To talk to MIT I had to sit at the MIT terminal. To bring in someone from Berkeley, I had to change chairs to another terminal," Taylor recalled in an interview with Marion Softky for *The Almanac*, an online publication.

As time passed, however, Taylor's annoyance spurred him to ponder ways in which he might improve the inefficient arrangement. Gradually, he began to envision a system in which existing computers might be electronically linked to one another. He believed that such a network would allow researchers in different parts of the country to share computer resources as well as the results of their work. "I wished I could connect someone at MIT directly with someone at Berkeley," he told Softky. "Out of that came the idea: Why not have one terminal that connects with all of them? That's why we built the ARPANET."

Taylor convinced ARPA to provide funding to create the world's first interactive computer network. This "ARPANET" network revolutionized communications and served as the foundation of the global Internet.

The ARPANET started out with four nodes in 1969 and grew rapidly over the next 25 years. Network access, which was initially limited to research universities and defense contractors, gradually expanded to reach other businesses and individuals. By the late 1980s over 150,000 computers were connected to the ARPANET, and exciting new applications were being created every day. Realizing that the network had grown beyond its initial purpose, the U.S. government decommissioned the ARPANET in 1990. This decision opened the ever-expanding network for commercial use, marking the official birth of the modern Internet.

Today, the network of computer networks known as the Internet connects millions of computers around the world and provides users with access to an incredible wealth of information resources. Robert H. Reid described the far-reaching impact of the Internet revolution in his book *Architects of the Web*:

> Although the Internet is [first and foremost] a technology, it is most significant as the stimulus and means to a new—and better—world, ultimately touching every facet of our lives…. Yes, the Internet is networks, software, computers, and other technologies; but more so, it is a catalyst of change, a new mass medium, a culture, a mindwarp, new things never before imagined. In the same manner that the world we live in is attributable to a major meteorite collision with the earth (which transformed our world from its previous era of the dinosaur), the Internet is a modern-day meteorite noteworthy not only because of itself, but rather because of the new world resulting from its aftermath…. [The Internet is] transforming the fundamental structure and nature of business, equalizing and empowering us as individuals and as a society, providing a new and better medium both for communicating and for enabling creativity, and challenging our conventional thoughts…. The transformations brought forth by the technology industry over the past 20 years, exemplified by the invention of the microprocessor, the advent of the personal computer, the rise of Microsoft and the fall of IBM, are mere gusts of wind compared to the tornado, the hurricane, and the tsunami wave of the Internet.

Chapter One

EARLY ORIGINS
OF THE INTERNET

In the early 1960s, when computers were scarce, expensive, and cumbersome, using a computer for communication was almost unthinkable. Even the sharing of software or data among users of different computers could be a formidable challenge. Before the advent of computer networks, a person who wanted to transfer information between computers usually had to carry some physical storage medium, such as a reel of magnetic tape or a stack of punch cards, from one machine to the other.

—Janet Abbate, *Inventing the Internet*

The history of the Internet can be traced back to the beginning of the Cold War. This was a period of intense political and military rivalry between the United States and the Soviet Union, which emerged as the world's two superpowers after World War II. Many in the U.S. feared that the Soviet Union and its allies were determined to force their Communist ideology on the rest of the world. Thus the U.S. and the Soviet Union became locked in the conflict known as the Cold War—a war defined not by open warfare, but by escalating hostilities between the two nations and the division of the major world governments into pro-U.S. and pro-Soviet blocs. The Cold War led the U.S. government to place an increased emphasis on national defense. Policymakers promoted the development of weapons and technology in hopes that the country would achieve a decisive military advantage over its Communist rival.

Leonard Kleinrock was an early developer and advocate of packet switching.

overlapped, leading to costly duplication of effort by researchers at different locations. Taylor felt that his researchers would benefit from sharing information and results with one another. With these ideas in mind, he became determined to create a system of electronic links among the ARPA research centers around the country. He convinced ARPA to fund research into computer networking technology, with the goal of linking all of the agency's mainframe computers into a single network.

Packet Switching

One of the technological breakthroughs that facilitated the development of the ARPANET was packet switching. Packets are units of electronic information or data, while switching refers to the way that packets are transmitted over a network. By the time Taylor launched the ARPA networking project in 1966, packet switching theory had been around for several years. Leonard Kleinrock, a computer science expert at the University of California-Los Angeles (UCLA), published the first paper on packet switching theory in July 1961. Two other researchers developed the idea independently around the same time: Paul Baran at the Rand Corporation and Donald Davies at the National Physical Laboratory in England.

Kleinrock and the other researchers believed that packet switching would allow data to flow more quickly and efficiently through computer networks. According to their theories, the computer sending the data would break the information into small packets. These packets could move quickly and separately through any number of network pathways. The computer receiving the packets would then reassemble the data. Under this theory of packet switching, information would continue to flow even if some paths to a particular destination became unavailable. The network would simply reroute data from computer to computer until it found a useable path to its destination. Packet switching, the researchers argued, would thus make computer networks more reliable by insulating them against problems in individual connected computers.

The researchers believed that packet switching would prove superior to circuit switching—the traditional single-path transmission method used in telephone lines. "When you make a phone call to your mother-in-law, and then talk to her on that phone line, whether you talk fast or slow or halt … in … the … middle, you tie up the phone line the whole time," researcher Frank Heart explained in *Nerds 2.0.1: A Brief History of the Internet.* "But computers tend to talk in little bursts when they talk to each other. So packet switching was a technique for intermixing bits of message all together with other people's messages and using a phone line efficiently so that you could transmit many, many, many different conversations all intertwined."

Davies introduced the packet switching theory to Larry Roberts, the computer scientist who had been selected by Bob Taylor to lead the ARPANET project. Roberts made the bold decision to test the method on the new network. "Packet switching was an experimental, even controversial method for transmitting data across a network," Janet Abbate explained in *Inventing the Internet.* "Its proponents claimed that it would increase the efficiency, reliability, and speed of data communications, but it was also quite complex to implement, and some communications experts argued that the technique would never work. Indeed, one reason the ARPANET became the focus of so much attention within the computer science community was that it represented the first large-scale demonstration of the feasibility of packet switching."

Another technical challenge to creating the ARPANET involved finding a way for different types of computers to communicate with each other. At this time, every type of mainframe computer used different operating systems—the basic software program, like Windows on many current PCs, that runs the entire computer. These varying operating systems presented a daunting obstacle to Taylor's information-sharing idea. It was as if every computer spoke an entirely different language.

To overcome this problem, Taylor and Roberts ultimately decided to build smaller computers, called Interface Message Processors (IMPs), specifically to translate information for the supercomputers. They planned to station an IMP between each mainframe and the network. The IMPs would handle both incoming and outgoing communication. "The IMPs were to be the hardware backbone of the ARPANET," Stephen Segaller explained in his book *Nerds 2.0.1*. "Each IMP would sit in front of its mainframe 'host,' communicating with the host in one direction, and the other network IMPs outside. The IMPs had to run the software that 'packetized' outgoing data, and reassembled incoming packets into coherent, ordered messages. The IMPs were connected to each other by leased 50-kilobit telephone lines. An IMP would be in constant touch with the traffic patterns on the network, and make a continuously changing assessment of the most efficient available route to send packets to their final destination."

Building the ARPANET

In 1968 ARPA managers finalized their plans for the structure of the ARPANET. ARPA sent out specifications to 140 computer companies across the United States and asked them to submit formal proposals for developing the network technology. After receiving bids from some of the largest and most prominent technology companies in the country, Taylor and Roberts hired Bolt Beranek and Newman (BBN), a small consulting firm based in Cambridge, Massachusetts, to develop key components of the ARPANET.

Although the decision to hire BBN surprised many industry experts, the small company had a history of hiring the best minds from nearby Harvard

Bob Kahn (fifth from left), Frank Heart (sixth from left) and the rest of the Bolt, Beranek & Newman (BBN) team that built the ARPANET.

University and the Massachusetts Institute of Technology (MIT). The team that developed the ARPANET technology featured several of the leading experts in the computer field, including Bob Kahn and Frank Heart. They successfully built the first IMP in nine months, delivering the refrigerator-sized machine to Len Kleinrock at the ARPA research center at UCLA in September 1969. Kleinrock enlisted the help of some of his graduate students—including Vinton Cerf, Steve Crocker, and Jonathan Postel—to write the software program that connected UCLA's mainframe to the IMP.

Once a second IMP was installed at the Stanford Research Institute (SRI) in October 1969, Kleinrock supervised the initial test of computer-to-computer communication over the ARPANET. He set up both voice and data connections over telephone lines between his lab at UCLA and the researchers at SRI. Kleinrock later expressed disappointment that the first message sent via packet-switching technology was not more profound. "All we tried to do was log on from our host to their host. Remember—we're engineers," he admitted in *Nerds 2.0.1*. "We typed in L. And we said, 'Did you get the L?' And he said, 'I got the L.' Typed the O. 'You get the O?' 'I got the O.' 'You get the G?' Crash! The system failed on the G. A couple hours later we successfully logged in, did some minimal things, and logged off. That was the first message on the Internet.... As I like to phrase it, the first message was 'Hello,' which is the way the two letters, L-O, sound."

The ARPANET was formally commissioned by the end of 1969 with just a few nodes. (In computing terminology, a node is a network intersection that features a device capable of processing or forwarding data transmissions.) It initially consisted of four nodes located at four separate locations: UCLA, SRI, the University of Utah, and the University of California at Santa Barbara. As the potential for network technology became clear, ARPA began expanding the ARPANET to reach other universities and scientific organizations. By 1971 the network included fifteen additional nodes, including one at the National Aeronautics and Space Administration (NASA). It did not take long for even the most skeptical researchers to discover the benefits of the ARPANET. "After [the network] came up, [researchers] found that they could exchange papers between Stanford and MIT very easily, and write papers jointly, which was great; and they suddenly found that this was a tremendous benefit rather than a tremendous harm," Larry Roberts remembered in *Nerds 2.0.1*.

Managing Growth and Development

The creators of the ARPANET took full advantage of the network's connections to some of the world's leading scientific research institutions. Instead of trying to protect proprietary information about the design and operation of the ARPANET, ARPA chose to share that information with all of its computer research centers. This policy was continued by Larry Roberts, who took over as director of IPTO when Taylor left in 1969. Roberts believed that a policy of information sharing would encourage computer experts across the country to contribute ideas to advance the networking technology. This early attitude led to a culture of sharing information and ideas that has persisted on the modern Internet. "A key to the rapid growth of the Internet has been the free and open access to the basic documents, especially the specifications of the protocols," wrote Barry Leiner and other ARPANET pioneers in their article "A Brief History of the Internet." "The beginnings of the ARPANET and the Internet in the university research community promoted the academic tradition of open publication of ideas and results."

In 1969 Kleinrock's graduate assistants began an ongoing effort to document the changing technological specifications for the ARPANET. As they worked to develop software for the IMPs, they sought input from experts at other ARPA research centers. Steve Crocker produced a memo describing his group's work and asking other researchers to provide suggestions for improvement. He titled this memo "Request for Comments" (RFC). It generated a number of responses and created a lasting method of cooperative network development (see "Steve Crocker Launches the 'Requests for Comments' Series," p. 144). "The effect of the RFCs was to create a positive feedback loop, with ideas or proposals presented in one RFC triggering another RFC with additional ideas, and so on," Leiner explained. "When some consensus (or at least a consistent set of ideas) had come together a specification document would be prepared."

As computer scientists adopted the RFC system for exchanging ideas, RFCs became the main method used to manage and document the development of the Internet. They have played an important role in the evaluation of new technical standards to the present day. One of Crocker's colleagues at UCLA, Jon Postel, served as the editor of the RFC series for more than two decades, ensuring that the documentation process remained consistent and fair.

Improving Communication

As the ARPANET expanded, the growing community of network users began developing new applications for the technology. "The ARPANET created an environment of both frustration and opportunity for its users," Janet Abbate noted in *Inventing the Internet*. "Using the network could be difficult, but a person with skill and determination (and there were many of these in the ARPANET community) could devise new applications with few restrictions. Thus, users had both the incentive and the ability to experiment with the system to make it better meet their needs."

One experiment that had a major impact on the ARPANET took place in 1971, when Ray Tomlinson, a computer engineer at Bolt Beranek and Newman,

The Evolution of Computer Technology

Computer hardware and software have undergone a revolution of their own over the past 60 years. Many of the developments in the computer and software industries facilitated the creation and rapid growth of the Internet.

The earliest computers—which were developed in the 1940s—were huge, room-sized machines that could be used only by trained professionals. Since they were very expensive and complicated to operate, they were used for advanced mathematical and scientific calculations rather than for communications or entertainment. These early computers were controlled using complex programming languages that were difficult to master. Data was typically entered using punch cards, or pieces of cardboard with holes in them that represented numerical values. The basis of their operation was binary codes—long strings of numbers consisting only of the digits 0 and 1, which dictated whether each electrical circuit in a series was switched on or off.

Beginning with the invention of the transistor in the 1950s, computers gradually became smaller, more powerful, and easier to operate. A major development occurred in 1968, with the introduction of the computer mouse and the "windows" environment. The earliest concept of "windows" was not the well-known Microsoft operating system of that name, but a general technique that allowed computer users to view different information on the screen at the same time. The founders of Apple Computer, Steve Jobs and Steve Wozniak, recognized the potential of the computer mouse and incorporated the technology into their computer systems in the late 1970s. It was several more years before the computer mouse became widely used on PCs.

By this time, advances in electronic circuitry and the development of memory chip technology made computers smaller and more affordable for businesses and individuals. Such advances also made computers more powerful. By the 1980s, for example, all of the processing power of the earliest room-sized computers would fit on a single memory chip that could be lifted with one finger.

A number of pioneers emerged during this time to develop new machines and software applications. One of the most famous of these individuals was Bill Gates, who co-founded Microsoft in 1975 with Paul Allen. In 1980 Microsoft was tapped to develop an operating system for the new IBM personal computer, or PC. The 16-bit operating system developed by Gates, called MS-DOS (for Microsoft Disk Operating System), required users to type in complicated series of text-based commands, sometimes using several keys simultaneously, like Control, Alt, and Function keys. These complicated commands made operating a computer difficult for all but the most dedicated users.

Other software manufacturers soon came up with their own operating systems. Xerox introduced the first graphical user interface (GUI) in the early 1980s. In contrast to the text-based DOS, which was difficult for non-experts to use, GUI-based operating systems allowed users to navigate their computer systems by using a mouse to point at and click on identifiable pictures, or icons. Apple adopted a GUI on its popular Macintosh computer system, which was introduced in 1984. The Mac made computers accessible to ordinary people with no knowledge of electronics or programming and helped create a market for personal computers.

Microsoft soon introduced its own GUI for PC machines, the popular Windows operating system. Microsoft Windows has been upgraded many times over the years—with the introduction of Windows 3.0, Windows 95, Windows 98, and Windows XP, for example—and eventually came to dominate the market for operating systems. Microsoft also developed a number of popular word processing, spreadsheet, and database software applications.

When the computer industry entered the 1990s, consumer and business demand for personal computers soared, boosted not only by proliferating software applications for recreational and professional purposes, but also by the exploding popularity of the Internet. Today, the Internet's tremendous popularity and influence continues to shape the evolution of the global computer and software industries.

introduced the first working electronic mail (e-mail) program. Tomlinson modified a network communications program he developed at BBN to work on the ARPANET. The original design of the ARPANET had included a mail function, but it was extremely difficult to use. Tomlinson's system was simple and efficient by comparison.

Under Tomlinson's scheme, each host computer connected to the network received a name, as did each individual user. To create a message, the sender just needed to specify the names of the user and the host computer that were intended to receive it. After scanning his keyboard, Tomlinson decided to separate the name of the user and the name of the host computer with "@," the typographical symbol for "at." This elegant touch made it easy for both people and computers to understand that the recipient of a message was "at" a different host system, rather than a user of the local network.

The first modern e-mail message on the ARPANET was a nonsense message Tomlinson created by dragging his finger across the keyboard. While working at BBN, he sent it to himself at a location outside the BBN offices. Within months of its introduction, his method of transferring mail files between network computers became one of the ARPANET's most popular features. In fact, e-mail messages accounted for 75 percent of traffic on the network within a year of the program's introduction.

The swift and near-universal embrace of e-mail in the ARPANET community was hardly a mystery. It was simply recognized for what it was: a fast, easy, and efficient new means of communicating and exchanging information. Network users could compose messages at their leisure and send copies to several recipients at once, regardless of whether those recipients were currently logged on to the ARPANET. E-mail made it easier for people to collaborate on scientific research or simply to keep in touch with distant friends. It generated a great deal of excitement and interest in the ARPANET and, over time, created a revolution in communication. "E-mail provided a new model of how people could communicate with each other, and changed the nature of collaboration, first in the building of the Internet itself and later for much of society," Leiner stated.

Connecting the Networks

By 1972 the ARPANET had expanded to include dozens of locations, yet the network was virtually unknown beyond the academic community. That changed in October, when Bob Kahn of BBN gave the first public demonstration of the ARPANET at the International Conference on Computer Communications in Washington, D.C. The technical performance consisted of logging into a computer at MIT from a terminal in Washington, then using the MIT host to run a computer program at UCLA, and finally sending the results back to a printer in Washington. The demonstration proved the value of packet-switching technology to a wider audience. "It was a 'who's who' of everybody in the field and it was just very eye-opening to a lot of people who did not know this was possible," Kahn recalled in *Nerds 2.0.1*. Afterward Kahn left BBN and moved to ARPA, eventually replacing Roberts as the director of IPTO.

The truck used by Bob Kahn and Vint Cerf in 1977 to prove the viability of data transmission across multiple types of networks.

By this time, the ARPANET was no longer the only packet-switching network in existence. A number of universities, companies, and government agencies—many using ARPA funding—adopted the technology to create different types of computer networks. One example was the Atlantic Packet Satellite Network, or SATnet, which relied upon satellite transmission of data. Similarly, researchers at the University of Hawaii created a packet radio transmission network called Alohanet. Unfortunately, the various networks were incompatible. "Each network was different, working exclusively within its own protocols, hardware, and software," Segaller explained. "A user could not send packets from one network to another, let alone through another to a third. They had vastly different technical characteristics."

Kahn and fellow researcher Vint Cerf (see Cerf biography, p. 120) realized that the ARPANET would become infinitely more valuable if it could communicate with these other computer networks. They coined the term "internetworking" to describe the challenge of interconnecting the various types of packet-switching networks. "Internetworking" was eventually shortened to "Internet." Kahn and Cerf came up with a plan to create an Internet that resembled the basic functioning of the ARPANET. They decided to place a "gateway" between each individual network and the larger Internet. These gateways would serve the same purpose as the IMPs in the ARPANET—breaking up information into packets, identifying the best route by which to send the packets, and reassembling packets into coherent messages. The only difference was that the gateways would need to translate messages between networks instead of between host computers. Kahn and Cerf outlined this plan, called "open-architecture networking," in 1973.

This system of internetworking offered a number of advantages. Perhaps most notably, it ensured that any type of network could be connected to the Internet, which left users free to design networks to meet their specific needs. "The Internet as we now know it embodies a key underlying technical idea, namely that of open architecture networking," Leiner noted. "In this approach, the choice of any individual network technology was not dictated by a particular network architecture but rather could be selected freely by a provider and made to internetwork with the other networks through a meta-level 'Internetworking Architecture.'" Another key benefit of the internetworking plan was that it provided for "scalability," or easy expansion without disrupting the flow of information between other networks.

The problem remaining for Kahn and Cerf was to develop a shared network protocol—a set of rules to define how the networks would communicate with each other. In May 1974 they unveiled their solution to the problem in an academic paper called "A Protocol for Packet Network Intercommunication." This paper detailed a set of network communication rules collectively known as Transmission Control Protocol (TCP). "TCP did much more than just set up a connection between two hosts: it verified the safe arrival of packets using acknowledgments, compensated for errors by retransmitting lost or damaged packets, and controlled the rate of data flow between the hosts by limiting the number of packets in transit," Abbate explained. "All this made it feasible to provide reliable communications over [unreliable networks]."

Over the next few years Kahn and Cerf continued working to refine their protocol. In 1976 Cerf joined Kahn at ARPA, which funded their work in hopes that it would lead to the development of a flexible, reliable command-and-control system to coordinate tactical operations by various branches of the military. In July 1977 Cerf conducted an elaborate test that demonstrated

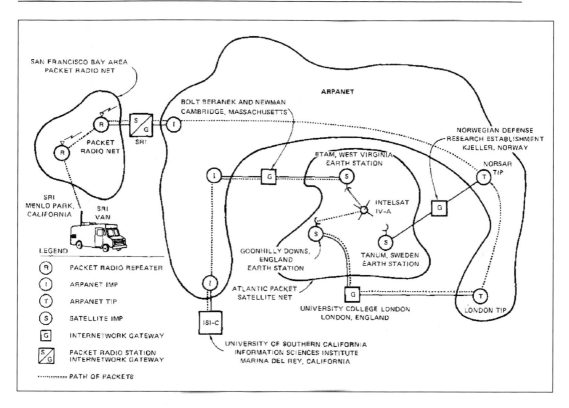

A diagram illustrating the path taken by Cerf and Kahn's historic July 1977 data transmission.

the possibilities of interconnected networks. He transmitted data over the Mobile Radio Network (from a truck on a California freeway) through an Internet gateway to the ARPANET. From there the data traveled to Europe through the Atlantic Satellite Network, across Europe on a land-based telephone line, and back to California via satellite. By the time it reached its destination, the data had traveled 94,000 miles around the world through several different types of networks. This success made Cerf even more excited about the promise of the technology, and over the next few years he became the industry's most visible and passionate advocate of the "internetworking" concept (see "Vinton Cerf Recalls the Early Development of the Internet," p. 135).

In 1978 Cerf and Kahn split their protocol into two parts, TCP and IP (Internetwork Protocol, later Internet Protocol). This split made the protocols less complicated and reduced the demands on gateways and individual networks. TCP became a host-to-host protocol, controlling the process of

19

packetizing and reassembling information between pairs of hosts. IP handled the routing of packets within the Internet, or the space between networks. Although it took a decade to complete the transition of the entire ARPANET to TCP/IP, these protocols stood the test of time and eventually became the basis for network communication on the modern Internet.

Giving Birth to the Internet

Until this point, the ARPANET had maintained a tenuous connection with the U.S. military. It had been created through the Department of Defense and had been intended as a tool for the U.S. military. But the expansion of the ARPANET to include other packet-switching networks launched a new round of growth for the network. In 1979 the National Science Foundation created the NSFnet, which started out as a research-oriented sister network to the ARPANET. One goal of NSFnet was to spread supercomputer access to researchers at all universities in the United States through internetworking technology. The NSF funded numerous connections to campuses across the country over the next few years. In 1983 the NSFnet was linked to the ARPANET. The broad public access that resulted from this union effectively ended the ARPANET's relationship with the U.S. military, which spun off its own separate network for defense purposes (MILNET) in 1983.

The mid-1980s saw the widespread introduction of personal computers to universities and businesses. Within a short time, many of these computers were being connected in local-area networks (LANs), computer networks that connect computers in a relatively small area, such as an office. Increasing numbers of these smaller networks were being connected to the ARPA Internet. In fact, the number of nodes on the ARPANET grew from 200 in 1981 to 2,000 in 1985. "Ever since the beginnings of ARPANET, other institutions, both public and private, had been building networks for research or communications purposes. The more there were, the more it made sense to hook more people in," Segaller wrote. "A wider range of scientific and research interests became connected: networking of the research community was no longer confined to computer scientists."

As the Internet expanded, however, concerns about security escalated. Much of the apprehension focused on "hackers"—people who would use their computer expertise to break into other people's computers. Hackers began accessing confidential software programs without permission, using their tech-

The U.S. Government Defines "Internet"

When the NSFnet was decommissioned in 1995, ending official U.S. government involvement in maintaining the infrastructure of the Internet, the Federal Networking Council (FNC) published its definition of the term "Internet." The following definition codified the use of the TCP/IP protocols, which had been invented by Vint Cerf and Bob Kahn two decades earlier, as the basis of network communications.

> Resolution: The Federal Networking Council (FNC) agrees that the following language reflects our definition of the term "Internet." "Internet" refers to the global information system that—(i) is logically linked together by a globally unique address space based on the Internet Protocol (IP) or its subsequent extensions/follow-ons; (ii) is able to support communications using the Transmission Control Protocol/Internet Protocol (TCP/IP) suite or its subsequent extensions/follow-ons; and (iii) provides, uses, or makes accessible, either publicly or privately, high-level services layered on the communications and related infrastructure described herein.

nological skills to break through safeguards like passwords and security codes. Some early hackers broke in to programs simply for the challenge, while others were motivated by a keen interest in figuring out how software worked. In fact, some early hackers left messages alerting programmers to weaknesses in the programs to allow them to correct these weaknesses. But others took advantage of the opportunity to steal information or vandalize programs. The first computer "virus"—a malicious program or piece of code that can damage or destroy individual computers or networks—was released on the Internet on November 1, 1988. Known as the Internet Worm, it disabled about 6,000 computers that served as network hosts before it was stopped (see "A Computer Scientist Describes the Internet Worm of 1988," p. 152).

By the late 1980s NSFnet was quickly becoming the backbone of the growing Internet. It offered easier connections and ran at speeds 25 times faster than the ARPANET. As the aging ARPANET lost favor with users, the government agency that had created it decided to move away from experiments in computer networking and concentrate on defense initiatives. ARPA managers also wanted to save the $14 million per year that the agency spent to keep the antiquated network up and running. Gradually, ARPANET sites were transferred to regional networks and the IMPs were turned off (Len Kleinrock kept the first IMP on display in his computer lab at UCLA for visitors).

On February 28, 1990, the ARPANET was officially decommissioned and NSFnet became the foundation of the Internet. In 1992 the National Science Foundation issued an "acceptable use" policy that expanded the network's purpose beyond research and development for the first time. The U.S. government ended its support of the network's infrastructure, and operation of the network started shifting to the private sector. These events, which opened up the network for commercial development, marked the birth of the modern Internet. Within a short time, over 1,000 fledgling Internet service providers (ISPs) had begun selling Internet access in local and regional markets. With the growth of these ISPs, more and more businesses and individuals were able to connect to the Internet. In 1995 the NSFnet reverted back to a research-oriented network, leaving interconnected private ISPs to provide the backbone of the Internet.

By the early 1990s, then, the Internet had evolved from "a single experimental network serving a dozen sites in the United States to a globe-spanning system linking millions of computers," Abbate wrote in *Inventing the Internet*. "It brought innovative communications techniques into the mainstream of networking practice, and it enabled a large number of Americans to experience the possibilities of cyberspace for the first time. By making distance interaction among different types of computers a commonplace reality, the Internet helped redefine the practice and the meaning of computing."

Chapter Two

INVENTION OF THE WORLD WIDE WEB

Prior to the Web, the Internet was ... a massive library of some of the most advanced information and discussion forums in the world from the leading research institutions, but locating and getting the information was obtrusively difficult. It was akin to walking down each aisle of a library, scanning each book just to figure out what is there, but doing all of this in the dark!

—Robert H. Reid, *Architects of the Web*

The Internet expanded rapidly in the late 1980s. But for a while, it seemed likely that use of the network would remain limited to computer experts and scientific researchers. The Internet provided access to millions of files of valuable information, but there was no easy method for users to find specific files. Even when the location was known, calling up files required users to type in a series of complicated commands. The difficulty in accessing information prompted some people to compare the Internet to a library in which all of the books were tossed into a giant pile.

Fortunately, the disorganized nature of the Internet inspired a number of users to create filing systems to help locate useful information. One of the earliest efforts was a program called Gopher. Gopher was created by two students at the University of Minnesota, Mark McCahill and Paul Lindner, who originally intended it to help organize files on the school's computer network. The program allowed students and faculty to organize their network files into a hierarchy of related topics. Then users of the system could select topics of interest from a series of text menus that resembled bulletin boards.

After a decade of research, Tim Berners-Lee unveiled the software and networking protocols that created the World Wide Web in 1990.

Gopher had limitations—it still required users to type in commands, for example, and could only handle text files. But it did facilitate the process of locating information. When McCahill and Lindner distributed the program over the Internet in 1991, thousands of other users downloaded it for free. Some of the earliest search engines, such as Archie and Veronica, were designed to work with Gopher. These programs allowed users to locate and retrieve information based on its content rather than its location.

Inventing the World Wide Web

A more enduring software application for finding information on the Internet was introduced in 1990. Known as the World Wide Web, it provided a means for linking related information to create a "single, global information space," as creator Tim Berners-Lee described it in his book *Weaving the Web* (see Berners-Lee biography, p. 107). "The basic idea of the Web is that of an information space through which people can communicate, but communicate in a special way: communicate by sharing their knowledge in a pool," he added in a 1999 speech. "The idea was not just that it should be a big browsing medium. The idea was that everybody would be putting their ideas in, as well as taking them out." His application also allowed programmers to incorporate graphics and sound in addition to text, which made the look and feel of the Internet more appealing to ordinary people (see "Tim Berners-Lee Remembers Inventing the World Wide Web," p. 166).

The World Wide Web took years to create. Berners-Lee first started developing the idea that eventually became the Web in 1980, while working as a computer software consultant at CERN (formerly Conseil Européen pour la Recherche Nucléaire), a laboratory for atomic research in Geneva, Switzerland. His original program, which he called Enquire, was designed to help him remember connections between the thousands of scientists and research projects at CERN. He soon expanded it to help the scientists locate files on their computer network.

Berners-Lee left CERN in 1981. When he returned three years later, he started thinking about the possibility of linking the information that was stored on computers all over the world. He wanted to invent a way for computers to function more like the human brain. "Computers were good at logical organizing and processing, but not random associations," he explained in *Weaving the Web*. "A computer typically keeps information in rigid hierarchies and matrices, whereas the human mind has the special ability to link random bits of data. When I smell coffee, strong and stale, I may find myself again in a small room over a corner coffeehouse in Oxford [where he went to college]. My brain makes a link, and instantly transports me there."

Over the next few years, Berners-Lee refined a technological concept known as hypertext, which provided a method for creating links between text documents. Hypertext uses embedded codes in documents that appear as highlighted text on the screen, so that when users click on the hypertext link they are transported to a web site containing related information. Berners-Lee used it to invent Hypertext Markup Language (HTML), a coding system that used tags to identify various elements in a document—including words, pictures, and sound—but let individual computers decide how to display the elements. In this way, HTML provided a shared format for documents that all computers could understand. It also allowed hypertext links to be embedded within documents. By clicking on a highlighted link, users could instantly jump to related information. Berners-Lee also invented the Hypertext Transfer Protocol (HTTP), a set of rules that guided the transfer of HTML files between computers on the Internet. He combined these innovations to create the World Wide Web, which effectively changed the Internet from a collection of separate networks into a web of interconnected networks.

Berners-Lee proposed the combination of software and networking protocols known as the World Wide Web in 1989. An early version was tested the following year, and an improved version was made available to the public in 1991. Programmers appreciated the fact that they could use HTML to combine words, pictures, and sound to create interesting documents, which became known as Web sites or Web pages. A number of new businesses formed to provide Web page design services for large companies. Before long, advances in software allowed ordinary Internet users to design Web pages without actually understanding the HTML code. The number of sites on the Web then started to grow at an exponential rate (see "The First World Wide Web Page with Hypertext Links," p. 164).

Creating Web Addresses

The final key to making Berners-Lee's hypertext system work on the Internet was to create a unique address for every document or site so that they could be linked together. At this point, computer addresses were made up of long strings of numbers. For users to communicate with another computer on the ARPANET, they would have to remember and type in these long strings of numbers. Berners-Lee wanted to create something simpler to use. He devised a Web address system he called Universal Resource Identifier (URI), which was later changed to Uniform Resource Locator (URL). URLs are textual names that identify the location of information on the Web, as in http://www.aol.com. URLs eliminated the need for users to remember numerical addresses.

Berners-Lee based his URL design on the Domain Name System (DNS), which had been created by Jon Postel and Paul Mockapetris in the early 1980s. They created DNS in order to provide a unique name for each host computer connected to the growing Internet. DNS designated a hierarchical structure for host names, beginning with the most specific identifier and ending with a general classification or domain. The original system divided Internet hosts into five "top-level domains" using three-letter abbreviations:

The Difference between the Internet and the World Wide Web

Today, the terms "Internet" and "World Wide Web" are often used interchangeably. Many people have lost sight of the fact that the World Wide Web is actually a program that runs on the vast computer network known as the Internet. Tim Berners-Lee, inventor of the Web, explained the difference on the home page for his World Wide Web Consortium, http://www.w3.org:

> The Internet (Net) is a network of networks. Basically it is made from computers and cables. What Vint Cerf and Bob Kahn did was to figure out how this could be used to send around little 'packets' of information.... A packet is a bit like a postcard with a simple address on it. If you put the right address on a packet, and gave it to any computer which is connected as part of the Net, each computer would figure out which cable to send it down next so that it would get to its destination. That's what the Internet does. It delivers packets—anywhere in the world, normally in well under a second....
>
> The Web is an abstract (imaginary) space of information. On the Net, you find computers. On the Web, you find documents, sounds, videos—information. On the Net, the connections are cables between computers. On the Web, connections are hypertext links. The Web exists because of programs which communicate between computers on the Net. The Web could not be without the Net. The Web made the Net useful because people are really interested in information (not to mention knowledge and wisdom!) and don't really want to have to know about computers and cables.

"com" for commercial sites; "org" for nonprofit organizations; "gov" for government agencies; "edu" for educational institutions; and "net" for networking groups. (A number of additional domains were added later, including two-letter country codes for international hosts.)

By dividing all hosts on the Internet into smaller domains, DNS ensured that no names were duplicated and that every host could obtain the name of every other host. Every domain contained one or more "name servers," or computers that maintained updated lists of all host names and addresses within the domain. When Berners-Lee created the URL system, he was adapting DNS to work with his new Web program. He added http:// and www, for instance, to identify the protocol and "space" he invented. Once the Web enjoyed widespread use, all URLs were registered with the Internet Network Information Center (InterNIC).

Surfing and Searching the Web

While the invention of the Web made it significantly easier for users to locate information and publish their own documents on the Internet, the application's search function still required users to type in text-based commands. "Although the Web's HTML language could translate and deliver both text and graphics from server to client, the on-screen process of searching the Web remained clunky," Stephen Segaller wrote in his book Nerds 2.0.1: *A Brief History of the Internet.* "What was needed was a graphical look and feel that would add user-friendliness to the sheer volume of materials that were now available."

The first graphical user interfaces (GUIs) for the Web, which appeared in 1993, were known as Web browsers. Web browser software enabled individual computers to interact with the World Wide Web. These "point-and-click" software programs retrieved pages from Web servers, interpreted the HTML codes, and displayed the information on the computer. They helped users identify the resources available on the Internet and presented HTML-formatted documents on their computer screens in an attractive and user-friendly manner. Today, the best-known Web browsers are Internet Explorer and Netscape Navigator. But the first widely accepted Web browser was Mosaic, created by student Marc Andreessen and several colleagues at the National Center for Supercomputing Applications (NCSA) at the University of Illinois at Urbana-Champaign (see Andreessen biography, p. 103). "What we were trying to do was just put a human face on the Internet. The Internet at that point was a tool for researchers and scientists," Andreessen explained in *Nerds 2.0.1.* "We wanted to take all the graphical user interface things that people were getting used to with word processors and spreadsheets and apply them to the Internet."

When Andreessen released an early version of Mosaic on the Web for free in March 1993, more than 40,000 copies were downloaded in the first month. By making it easy and fun for ordinary people to browse the Web, Mosaic gave the Internet a new mass-market appeal. "Mosaic just may have been the most important computer application ever," wrote Steven Levy in *Newsweek*. "Mosaic was an instant success online. Within six months more than a million people had downloaded it. A cycle of motion had begun. Before Mosaic, there were only a few hundred Web sites. But when huge numbers of people were able to access colorful pages, there was incentive to create innovative sites. That provided Web surfers with more reason to stay online."

Andreessen left school in 1994 to develop Mosaic into a commercial enterprise. He formed a company called Netscape and introduced an

Marc Andreessen, co-founder of the Web browser Mosaic (later Netscape Navigator), became a symbol of the emerging "Internet economy" in the 1990s.

improved version of the browser, which became known as Netscape Navigator. Navigator featured new security measures, improved graphics, and greater speed than Andreessen's original program. It was also compatible with Windows and Macintosh operating systems, in addition to the Unix-based computer systems he had used at NCSA. In 1995 Netscape held a historic initial public stock offering that made Andreessen an instant multi-millionaire. Netscape's success is largely credited with giving rise to a rush of Internet start-up businesses that became known as the "dot.com" boom.

As the number of Web sites grew, sorting through them became an increasingly cumbersome process. A number of programmers addressed this problem by creating search engines, or software programs that sort through information on the Web and create lists of sites that meet search criteria. One of the earliest search engines to gain widespread attention was Yahoo!, which was created in

Students at the University of New Hampshire surf the Internet during a computer lab class.

1994 by Jerry Yang and David Filo, engineering students at Stanford University (see biographies on Yang and Filo, p. 124). It began as a list of their own favorite Web sites, but the following year they transformed it into a business. Dozens of competing search engines were developed over the next few years, including AltaVista, Excite, and Lycos. Google, founded by Stanford students Sergey Brin and Larry Page, was the first search engine to rank Web sites by the number of links they receive from other sites, based on the supposition these pages are considered more valuable by users (see biographies on Brin and Page, p. 112).

Transforming the Internet

As creating and accessing Web sites became easier, countless individuals, businesses, and other organizations were inspired to build their own home pages. The White House opened its Web site in 1993, for instance, and the government of Japan went online the following year. In the meantime, affordable home computers and commercial online services became widespread.

Such online services as America Online (AOL), Compuserve, and Prodigy made it easier for ordinary people to access the Internet. By 1994 AOL, which had been founded only a few years earlier by Jim Kimsey and Steve Case, boasted one million members (see Case biography, p. 115). Although these services started out offering users access to private networks, demand soon grew for unfettered access to the broader Internet. People increasingly used the Internet to play games, share hobbies, shop, listen to music, conduct research, and do any number of other things.

As the Web made the Internet more useful and interesting for ordinary people, the number of users worldwide increased at an amazing rate—from 45 million in 1996, to 150 million in 1999, to 300 million in 2000, to 800 million in 2004. In the meantime, the number of Web sites these users could access grew from 3,000 in 1994, to 30 million in 2001, to 4.2 billion in 2004. A decade after the introduction of the World Wide Web, over half the U.S. population relied on the Internet for sending and receiving electronic mail; participating in online chats; entering contests; getting updates on the news and weather; or searching for information about products, services, events, and travel destinations. In this way, the Web transformed the Internet from a vast computer network into a global information resource.

"The Web would fundamentally change the Internet, not by expanding its infrastructure or underlying protocols, but by providing an application that would lure millions of new users," Janet Abbate explained in her book *Inventing the Internet*. "The Web also changed people's perception of the Internet: Instead of being seen as a research tool or even a conduit for messages between people, the network took on new roles as an entertainment medium, a shop window, and a vehicle for presenting one's persona to the world."

Chapter Three

HOW THE
INTERNET WORKS

———⟨⟨⟨⟨ ∩ ⟩⟩⟩⟩———

The Internet is at once a worldwide broadcasting capability,
a mechanism for information dissemination, and a medium
for collaboration and interaction between individuals and
their computers without regard for geographic location.

—Barry Leiner, "A Brief History of the Internet"

While many people use the Internet every day, few people understand how it works. The Internet is a vast network of computer networks that stretches around the world. Although each of the smaller networks that make up the Internet uses its own machines and software, all of these networks are able to communicate with each other through standard protocols, or rules, that define how the larger network operates. These protocols are like a common language shared by various types of computers and networks. Some analysts have described the communication between different types of networks that takes place on the Internet as being similar to a person from France and a person from Spain speaking to one another in English.

Ensuring the free flow of information among networks connected to the Internet requires a great deal of cooperative effort. For this reason, many people believe that the Internet must be under the control of a central organization or governing body. In reality, however, there is no centralized source of control over the functioning of the Internet. Instead, a number of different groups—including the Internet Society, the Volunteer Internet Engineering Task Force (IETF), and the World Wide Web (W3) Consortium—help guide its growth and development with input from computer scientists, software engineers, network managers, commercial enterprises, and other interested

A Michigan fourth-grader works on an assignment in his school computer lab.

parties. This culture of collaboration and sharing of ideas has existed since the earliest days of the Internet, when the graduate students who wrote the software for the first Interface Message Processors (IMPs) started the Request for Comments (RFC) system.

Since no one really owns or controls the Internet, some people wonder who pays to maintain it. The local networks that provide the basis for the Internet can be found in companies, universities, and government agencies around the world, and these various organizations generally provide the funding to support their own networks. In many cases, the organizations collect money from network users in the form of taxes, tuition, or fees for online services. It thus may be fair to say that users ultimately provide the funding for the Internet.

Packet Switching

One of the fundamental concepts underlying the operation of the Internet is packet switching. All information sent over the Internet is broken into small pieces—less than 1,500 characters long—called packets. These packets are sent separately through any number of different routes to their final destination, where they are reassembled in the proper order. There is no single, dedicated connection that carries information from one computer to another over the Internet.

Some analysts have compared the packet-switching method of delivering information over the Internet with the operation of the U.S. Postal Service. When an individual customer sends a letter, it is mixed in with other letters and transported to the local post office. Then all the mail is sorted and sent to its final destination using the most efficient route. Similarly, an individual computer sends packets of information to a local network server or the host computer of an Internet Service Provider (ISP). Then the packets are mingled together with packets from other sources and transported through many different networks and computers. By the time the packets reach their destination, they may have been transferred through satellites, fiber-optic cables, Integrated Services Digital Network (ISDN) telephone lines, high-speed Digital Subscriber Line (DSL) connections, and wireless networks—all of which act like mail trucks and planes transporting information over the Internet.

The numerous small, local networks that make up the Internet are grouped together to form regional networks. These regional networks are connected together by Internet "backbones," or high-capacity lines that can carry huge amounts of data. Standing between these networks are powerful computers called routers. Routers read the "address" inside packets of information and decide how best to send each packet toward its final destination. In this way, routers work like a regional post office that sorts mail and places it on the appropriate trucks and planes. Though not all routers on the Internet have a direct connection to each other, every router has the ability to evaluate its available connections and determine the most efficient route to advance a packet toward its destination.

Protocols

All computers connected to the Internet operate using the same set of rules, or protocols. Transmission Control Protocol (TCP) is responsible for breaking down information into packets and then reassembling the packets in the proper order. Internet Protocol (IP) controls the process of addressing packets so that routers know where to send them. Together these protocols

Students study in the technology training center of an elementary school on the Spokane Indian Reservation in Washington state.

are known as TCP/IP. These days, all new personal computers come equipped with software that understands TCP/IP. The software is called Winsock in PC machines and MacTCP in Macintosh machines. This software functions like an interpreter between the computer and the Internet.

Every computer connected to the Internet has a unique IP address. This address consists of four numbers—each one lower than 256—separated by periods (an example of an IP address might be 66.139.79.225). Internet Protocol puts the IP addresses of the sender and recipient on each packet of information, sort of like an envelope, so that every other computer on the Internet will know where the packet came from and where it is going.

Though IP addresses are easy for computers to understand, human users of the Internet found it difficult to remember these long strings of numbers. Internet developers solved this problem by creating the Domain Name System (DNS), which made the Internet more convenient by allowing people to use plain English words to locate individual computers on the network. The DNS designated a structure for host names, beginning with the specific identifier and followed by a period (dot) and a general classification or domain. The system originally divided Internet hosts into five "top-level domains" using three-letter abbreviations: "com" for commercial sites; "org" for nonprofit organizations; "gov" for government agencies; "edu" for educational institutions; and "net" for networking groups. A number of additional domains were added later, including two-letter country codes for international hosts. By dividing all hosts on the Internet into smaller domains, the DNS ensured that no names were duplicated and that every host could obtain the name of every other host. Every domain contains one or more "name servers," or computers that maintain updated lists of all host names and addresses within the domain. The name servers also handle the task of translating the Web site names into numerical IP addresses.

Communicating on the Internet

Electronic mail, commonly known as e-mail, is one of the most popular features of the Internet. E-mail messages are broken down into small packets and transmitted across the Internet in the same way as other data. In 2001 the Internet carried nearly 10 billion e-mail messages per day, and this number has increased every year since. E-mail provides a quick and relatively inexpensive way for people to keep in touch with friends, relatives, academic colleagues, and business associates in distant locations around the world.

An e-mail address typically consists of a user name and a host name, separated by "@"—the typographical symbol for "at." (An example of an e-mail address might be user99@aol.com.) A large number of individual computer users can access information and send messages using the same network server or host. In the case of home computers, the host is usually an Internet Service Provider—like America Online (AOL), Microsoft Network (MSN), or a local telephone or cable TV company—that provides access in exchange for a monthly fee. When a home computer is connected to the Internet through an ISP, it uses one of a shared pool of IP addresses belonging to the ISP. Each user of that computer can establish a unique e-mail address that will be recognized by the host, which will route messages to the home computer when it is connected to the Internet.

Most computers use e-mail software packages to manage mail. These programs allow users to compose and read e-mail, save and organize sent and

The Inventor of E-Mail

Ray Tomlinson

In 1971 a young computer engineer at Bolt Beranek and Newman (BBN) named Ray Tomlinson devised an ingenious—and now ubiquitous—new method of communication called electronic mail, or e-mail. Today, his invention is as familiar to many Americans and other people around the world as the television, the telephone, and other trappings of modern society.

Tomlinson's invention stemmed from his company's work on the ARPANET, precursor to the Internet. He has freely acknowledged that it originated not out of any officially sanctioned work, but rather out of his own conviction that the capacity to send messages electronically to far-flung destinations would be "neat." With that in mind, he devised a "send message" program that worked first on a local system, and then across all ARPANET nodes. He

The World Wide Web

The World Wide Web is essentially a sophisticated program that runs on the global computer network known as the Internet. Its introduction in the early 1990s helped change the Internet from a collection of separate networks into a web of interconnected servers. The World Wide Web consists of billions of interactive documents called Web pages. Web pages can incorporate words, pictures, sound, and other elements. They are generally built using Hypertext Markup Language (HTML). This coding system uses embedded commands or tags to identify the various elements in a document, but lets individual computers decide how to display these elements. In this way, HTML provides a shared format for documents that all computers can understand. As a result, anyone with basic computer skills can build a Web page using HTML and post it on a Web server using File Transfer Protocol (FTP) software.

later estimated that his e-mail program took him no more than six hours to complete, spread over a week or two "when I had a spare moment." He also indicated that he came up with the "@" symbol to designate remote mailbox destinations after "30 to 40 seconds of thought."

As it turned out, ARPA Director Larry Roberts liked Tomlinson's system so well that he began using e-mail for all his correspondence. Researchers eager for ARPA grants had no choice but to follow suit, and before long electronic mail was entrenched in the fast-growing ARPANET. And since that time, it has grown in tandem with the larger Internet phenomenon to the point that it is regarded as an essential tool in business and personal communication alike.

Tomlinson, who continues to work at BBN Technologies, acknowledges wistfully that it would have been nice if his innovation had brought him an infusion of personal wealth. But like many other pioneers in the development of the Internet, his efforts were not motivated by money, and he is proud of the enduring contribution he made to modern communications. "The cases where it has opened up new avenues of communication between people has been gratifying," he told *Darwin Magazine*. "I have received a number of e-mails from individuals who have found it to be a godsend in getting in touch with people and building a sense of community."

The term "Web site" usually refers to a collection of related documents or pages. The first or top page in a Web site, called the home page, generally acts as a table of contents to help guide users to information available elsewhere on the site. The various pages in a Web site are connected to each other using hypertext links—embedded HTML tags that identify the location of each page. On the computer screen, these links appear as highlighted words, symbols, or pictures. By clicking on a highlighted link, users can instantly jump to another Web page. Many Web sites also include links to other Web sites that feature related information.

Every Web page occupies a unique location on the Internet. Connected computers find and retrieve pages on the Web using a textual address called a Uniform Resource Locator (URL). The first part of each URL identifies the protocol that will be used to transfer information from the server—usually Hyper-

Internet pioneers Vinton Cerf, Lawrence Roberts, Robert Kahn, and Tim Berners-Lee pose for assembled media at a 2002 scientific award ceremony.

text Transfer Protocol (http). It is followed by the name of the Internet resource where the information resides—usually the World Wide Web (www). Next comes the IP address of the Web server or host computer that contains the page, including the three-letter domain abbreviation. An extended URL might also include a directory name, a document name, a date, and other information. (An example of a URL for a Web site might be http://www.isoc.org/internet/history.)

Individual computers interact with the World Wide Web using browser software, like Microsoft Internet Explorer or Netscape Navigator. These programs retrieve pages from Web servers, interpret the HTML codes, and display the information on the computer. Web browsers also automatically convert the text-based URLs into numerical IP addresses, since computers understand numbers rather than textual names.

Since the World Wide Web contains billions of pages, users need sophisticated tools to shift through the available information to find what they need.

The two main methods of searching for information on the Web are indexes and search engines. Indexes provide lists of Web sites broken down into categories. Users can select categories to narrow their search until they find the information they want. About.com is one frequently used Web index. Search engines are databases containing subject and keyword information for millions of Web pages. They are created using "spiders," special programs that collect information about the resources available on the Internet. Users begin a search by typing terms into the search engine. The search engine compares the terms to the information in its database and returns a list of documents that contain the terms. All of the major search engines create their databases and return search results in different ways. There is also meta-search software, which enables users to search through the databases of a variety of search engines simultaneously.

Benefits and Risks of Connecting to the Internet

The Internet is a valuable resource, facilitating communication and information sharing between people and organizations around the world. It allows users to access up-to-date news and weather forecasts, explore the collections of distant libraries and museums, sell goods and services, shop from the comfort of their homes, share interests through discussion groups and chat rooms, keep in touch with friends, collaborate on work projects, contact experts for help with problems, play adventure and role-playing games, and conduct business, academic, and personal research on thousands of topics.

For all its positive contributions, however, the Internet also exposes users to potential dangers every time they go online. The open, public nature of the network not only allows for the free exchange of information, but also leaves every computer connected to it vulnerable to hackers, viruses, and invasions of privacy. Hackers can go through high-speed Internet connections to gain access to home computers or corporate networks. They can take advantage of such access to steal information, damage data, or use the computer system for illegal purposes, such as sending spam or launching attacks on ISPs or Web sites. The main means of protection against Internet hackers are firewalls—combinations of hardware and software that create barriers to prevent unwanted traffic from flowing between a computer or network and the Internet.

The Internet is also a common source of viruses and worms—malicious programs that cause varying degrees of damage to computers and networks.

Students work in a school computer lab in Lahore, Pakistan.

Internet users can expose their machines to viruses by downloading files or opening infected e-mail attachments. Worms are usually disguised as helpful programs or files. When they are opened or run, however, they spread from computer to computer across a network. Worms can overwhelm systems with mail or unnecessary tasks to the point that they "crash." Likewise, viruses can corrupt data, programs, and system files so that computers behave oddly or stop working altogether. Antivirus software provides the best protection against viruses and worms. This type of program typically scans incoming e-mail and downloads and warns the user when malicious programs are detected. Most antivirus programs are able to quarantine or eradicate viruses and worms so that they are unable to damage the computer system.

There are still more potentially harmful programs. Spyware is a type of program that runs behind the scenes on a computer, usually without the knowledge of the user. Spyware is usually downloaded from the Internet by accident along with a useful program. Once installed, it tracks which Web sites the user visits and regularly reports back to a central spyware Web site. This site creates a profile of the computer user's surfing habits and takes advantage of the information to deliver self-launching advertisements (commonly known as pop-up ads) targeted specifically toward the user's interests. For example, a user who frequently visited Web sites devoted to financial planning might receive pop-up ads relating to banking and investments. Many Internet users find pop-up ads annoying and feel that spyware represents an invasion of their privacy. The only way to remove spyware from a computer is to employ software programs that are specially designed to kill it.

Chapter Four

OPENING THE INTERNET FOR COMMERCE

—◆—

The Web ... has no geography, no landscape. It has no distance. It has nothing natural in it. It has few rules of behavior and fewer lines of authority. Common sense doesn't hold there, and uncommon sense hasn't yet emerged. No wonder we're having trouble figuring out how to build businesses in this new land.

—David Weinberger, *Small Pieces Loosely Joined*

T he creation of the World Wide Web made navigating the Internet infinitely easier. But the Web's public introduction in 1991 was only the first step in transforming the Internet into a global information resource. In fact, the Web grew rather slowly during the first few years of its existence. Although hyperlink technology enabled users to jump instantly to Web pages with related information, this offered limited benefits as long as the total number of Web sites remained modest. As a result, the Web still accounted for only one percent of all Internet traffic in 1993.

Around this time, however, businesses became increasingly aware of how Internet technology could help them connect with customers and sell goods and services. They successfully pressed the U.S. government to make the network available for commercial use. Opening the Internet for commerce led to a marked increase in public awareness and interest; it also led to a rapid proliferation of sites that turned the Web into a worldwide shopping mall. But this metamorphosis might never have happened were it not for several developments that occurred in the mid-1990s. "In hindsight one can easily say that the commercialization of the Internet was inevitable, as people often do when looking back on the confusing tangle of facts as they happened," Paul E. Ceruzzi acknowledged in his book *A History of Modern Computing*. "In fact such a transformation could not have happened without jumping over a number of hurdles, social, political, and technical."

Making Commerce an Acceptable Use

Perhaps the most important factor in opening the Internet to commerce was the U.S. government's decision to turn over responsibility for the operation of the network to private enterprises. The U.S. government had started funding research into computer networking in the 1960s through its Advanced Research Projects Agency (ARPA). ARPA's research produced the ARPANET—the original ancestor of the modern Internet. In the 1980s the federal government assigned the National Science Foundation (NSF) responsibility for spreading network access to research institutions across the country. The NSF built its own network, NSFnet, which replaced the aging ARPANET when it was decommissioned in 1990.

When the U.S. government ran the network, no commercial use was allowed. Although large corporations were connected to the ARPANET from the beginning, their use was initially restricted to research and development for federal projects. When the NSF took over responsibility for computer networking research, agency officials were aware that corporate use of the network was growing rapidly. Personal computers had become commonplace in business by this time. Many of these computers were connected via local-area networks (LANs), and increasing numbers of these smaller networks were connected to the Internet. Since the NSF's network was funded by taxpayers, however, the officials wanted to make sure that the businesses did not use the network for advertising or other commercial purposes.

With these concerns in mind, the NSF issued an "Acceptable Use Policy" outlining the activities that were permitted on NSFnet. "NSF Backbone services are provided to support open research and education in and among U.S. research and instructional institutions, plus research arms of for-profit firms when engaged in open scholarly communication and research," the policy read. "Use for other purposes is not acceptable." Although the policy allowed companies to use the network to announce the availability of new products and to disseminate technical information about them, it prohibited advertising and "extensive use for private or personal business."

But then the World Wide Web emerged and made the Internet more accessible for ordinary people. Soon, some analysts began to foresee the technology's commercial potential. Several U.S. political leaders stepped forward to propose expanding use of the Internet beyond scientific research, making the technology available to businesses and to the general public. One of these officials, Congressman Rich Boucher of Virginia, introduced an amendment to legislation in 1992 that authorized the NSF to support computer networks that were used for other purposes besides research and education. Boucher's amendment effectively overturned the NSF's Acceptable Use Policy and opened up NSFnet for commercial use.

Another early champion of expanding government support for computer networking was Senator Al Gore of Tennessee, who later became vice president in 1993 under President Bill Clinton. In the Senate, Gore served as chairman of the Commerce Subcommittee on Science, Technology, and Space. As early as 1988 he proposed developing an "Information Superhighway," which he envisioned as a high-speed computer network that would facilitate collaboration and information sharing among the nation's scientists and engineers. He also sponsored the High-Performance Computing Act of 1991, which authorized the creation of the National Research and Education Network (NREN) under the NSF. NREN was intended to link educational institutions, government agencies, and businesses through high-performance computer systems.

Gore built upon this legislation by sponsoring the Information Infrastructure and Technology Act of 1992, which transferred responsibility for the operation of NREN from the NSF to telecommunications companies and other private interests. By privatizing this government-funded network, Gore contributed to opening the Internet for commercial activity (see "Al Gore and the Creation of the Internet," p. 48). The 1992 bill sought to apply the technology developed through the High-Performance Computing Act to schools, libraries, health care facilities, and manufacturing industries. "To help increase U.S. competitiveness and create jobs for Americans, the technology developed by the High-Performance Computing Act must be moved from the laboratories into the marketplace where it can be used," Gore stated in a press release announcing his introduction of the legislation. "This new bill will make sure this happens by developing practical applications for advanced technologies and high-performance computing." Gore remained committed to expanding Internet usage after he became vice president. For example, he ensured that the White House and all federal agencies set up their own Web sites.

Al Gore and the Creation of the Internet

The 2000 presidential campaign pitted Democratic nominee Vice President Al Gore against Texas Governor George W. Bush, the Republican nominee. During the campaign, the vice president was harshly criticized for falsely claiming to have invented the Internet. Political opponents seized upon this charge as evidence that Gore was prone to outlandish exaggerations, and by most accounts it hurt his campaign for the presidency.

In reality, however, Gore never claimed to have created the Internet. The false charge against Gore appears to have stemmed from a 1999 interview with Cable News Network (CNN), in which he stated that "during my service in the United States Congress, I took the initiative in creating the Internet." But this assertion is a far different claim than outright invention of the Internet. In fact, the "invented the Internet" phrase that Gore was alleged to have spoken actually first appeared in a Republican Party press release; it was then uncritically picked up and publicized by the national news media.

Gore's actual statement is regarded by many Internet historians as a fairly accurate description of his contribution to the development of the technology. They note that he championed the concept of an "information superhighway" in numerous remarks and speeches long before most of his Congressional colleagues had the slightest inkling about the new technology. Even more importantly, such Internet luminaries as Vinton Cerf have publicly confirmed the importance of Gore's legislative work in helping transform the ARPANET into the modern Internet.

The U.S. government completed the process of relinquishing its control over the Internet in 1995, when the NSFnet reverted back to a research-oriented network. That left the interconnected private Internet Service Providers (ISPs) to provide the backbone of the Internet. As the government gave up its claims, businesses large and small started to view the Internet as an exciting new way to sell their products and services. The first commercial Web sites started appearing in 1994, and before long commerce became a dominant feature of the Internet.

Adapting Technology to Meet Business Needs

At the same time that the federal government was stepping aside to open up the Internet for commercial use, several new technologies emerged to help both businesses and individuals get more out of their interactions with the network. One such technological advance was the introduction of Web browser software, like Mosaic, that made it easy and even fun to access information on the Web. Mosaic allowed users to interact with the Web through a graphical interface rather than through text-based commands. Unlike other software that ran only on the UNIX operating system used in the world of scientific research, Mosaic was also compatible with the Windows and Macintosh systems most commonly found on home and business computers.

Web browsers helped popularize the Web and fundamentally changed the relationship between people and computers. "Before browsers, the traditional on-screen desktop reflected the essentially static state of the computing environment: users and machines locked together in a virtual cubicle," Steven Levy wrote in an article for *Newsweek*. "But beginning with Mosaic, the metaphor changed. Using a computer didn't mean sitting but moving—traveling or 'surfing' on a sea of information that existed beyond your personal horizon."

Search engines were another technological advance that contributed to the commercialization of the Web. Yahoo!, the first modern search engine, was introduced in 1994. Created by Stanford University students Jerry Yang and David Filo, Yahoo! started out as a list of their favorite Web sites. But it soon grew into a Web "portal," a Web site dedicated to helping people find information on the Web. Many people praised Yahoo! for providing a "human touch" that made users feel more comfortable in visiting the Web. Thanks in part to browsers and search engines, the Web became the focus of the growing commercial use of the Internet.

The third technological advance that aided commercial development of the Internet was the introduction of the Java programming language in early 1995. Developed by Sun Microsystems, Java provided the means for businesses to create Web sites that would help attract customers and differentiate themselves from the competition. "At the precise moment that commercial uses were being allowed on the Internet, and as the World Wide Web made navigating easy, along came Java: a language that enabled Web designers to put the 'sizzle' in their offerings," Ceruzzi explained. "Java quickly became the means by which Web designers could give their pages animation, movement, and interactivity. It caught on because a program written in Java could run on nearly any computer, large or small, from any vendor that was connected."

Launching Electronic Commerce

Once the political and technical pieces were in place, commercial use of the Internet grew quickly. Businesses increasingly viewed the Internet as a potentially lucrative new way to sell their products and services, and the Web began to evolve from a communications tool into a center for advertising and shopping. One of the first successful e-commerce sites was an online bookstore called Amazon.com. Launched by entrepreneur Jeff Bezos in 1995, the site started out processing 100 orders per day during its first year in business. By 2000 it was processing 100 orders per minute. Another early Web-based business was the online auction site eBay, which also first appeared in 1995. eBay began turning a profit shortly after its introduction, and by 2001 the site hosted an average of 7 million ongoing auctions at a time.

The success of these early e-commerce sites attracted attention in the world of business, and before long thousands of companies were scrambling to create their own Web sites. Many existing businesses found that the Internet offered opportunities to enhance customer service and streamline operations. "The Internet is stimulating wholesale changes in essentially every industry and every business," Robert H. Reid wrote in *Architects of the Web*. "The interactive, personalizable, and communications capabilities of the Internet enables businesses to drive their operations around customers—including establishing priceless customer relationships—while providing more service and knowledge than was ever before possible. As if that wasn't enough bang for the buck, the Internet provides these breakthrough benefits at lower cost and greater customer involvement and satisfaction."

In addition, Internet entrepreneurs created a wave of new businesses to take advantage of the technology. People rushed to claim the new opportunities that the Web presented, hopeful that establishing an early presence would enable their companies to grow quickly. Some of these companies existed only online, as opposed to traditional "brick and mortar" stores. One example of such a business was Napster, which was launched by college student Shawn Fanning in 1999. The foundation of Napster was a file-sharing software program that enabled users to exchange music files over the Inter-

Jeff Bezos launched the Internet bookstore Amazon.com in 1995.

net. Within a year of its release, the program was being used by over 25 million people around the world. It started out as a free service but soon received so much investor interest that Fanning turned it into a business.

As the number of Web-based companies grew at an exponential rate, however, some experts warned that many of the new enterprises were built on questionable foundations. According to these analysts, the feverish pursuit of Web-based profits had led both companies and investors to disregard—or at least discount—basic principles of business operation and planning. "This growth has fostered a mind-warping mentality and behavior for Internet companies," Reid explained. "Tossing aside just about every experience-honed tenet of business to build businesses in a methodical fashion, Internet businesses have adopted a grow-at-any-cost, without-any-revenue, claim-as-much-market-real-estate-before-anyone-moves-in approach to business."

Even critics, however, concurred with the universal feeling that the commercialization of the Internet was having a far-reaching impact on society. "The Internet ... was no longer only a facet of computing technology; now it

Shawn Fanning, creator of the controversial Napster music-sharing Web business.

was part of entertainment, consumer spending, and popular culture," Ceruzzi noted. "The Internet had fused computing with the mainstream of social life in America."

The "Browser Wars"

As commercial interests began to dominate the Internet, many companies engaged in heated competition to win over online customers. The best-known example of such competition involved two highly successful companies in the world of computer software and Internet applications: Microsoft Corporation and Netscape Communications. Their battle for control of the market for Web browsers, which began in 1995, had a tremendous impact not only on the Internet, but also on the stock market and the American economy.

Microsoft Corporation, founded by Bill Gates and Paul Allen in 1975, had built a dominant position in personal computer software by the 1990s. One of its most successful products was the Windows operating system, which offered PC users a graphical user interface (GUI) similar to that found on Apple computers. The company forged agreements with computer manufacturers so that Windows was installed as standard equipment on 90 percent of all new PCs. Microsoft also developed software applications like Excel (a spreadsheet program) and Word (a word-processing program) that became very popular among computer users. With time, the company developed a suite of programs, Microsoft Office, that covered most users' computer software needs. Over the years, Microsoft earned a reputation as an innovative and aggressive competitor. Yet Microsoft responded somewhat slowly to the growth of Internet software and e-commerce in the mid-1990s.

Netscape Communications grew out of the extremely successful Mosaic Web browser. Mosaic was developed by Marc Andreessen and several colleagues at the National Center for Supercomputing Applications (NCSA) at the University of Illinois. In early 1994 Andreessen established a partnership

Steve Case (left) of America Online (AOL) and Bill Gates (right) of Microsoft established a mutually beneficial business alliance in the late 1990s.

with Jim Clark, founder of Silicon Graphics, with the goal of marketing his browser invention. They formed Netscape Communications, hired several of the best programmers from the NCSA, and introduced an improved version of the browser—called Netscape Navigator—to the public in September 1994.

On August 8, 1995, Netscape offered shares of stock to the public for the first time. The company's stock price started out at $28 per share. By the end of the first day of trading, the price had been bid up to $58 per share by eager investors who believed that Navigator would control the market for Web browsers. Within a few months, Netscape stock was selling for $150 per share. The news was suddenly full of stories about people who had invested in the stock at the original price and become millionaires overnight. The excitement over Netscape's historic initial public offering (IPO) generated a great deal of investor interest in other Internet companies. Many Web-based businesses followed Netscape's lead and held successful IPOs, which contributed to an overall rise in the value of the stock market. This period in history became known as the "dot.com" boom, after the three-letter domain abbreviation used for commercial Web sites.

Prior to Netscape's IPO, Microsoft had concentrated on improving its Windows operating system and introducing new software applications. Although Gates had watched the commercialization of the Internet with interest, he hesitated to join the fray. But Netscape's successful stock offering convinced Microsoft to take action. A short time later, Gates distributed a passionate memo to his employees, asking them to respond to the challenge presented by "The Internet Tidal Wave." He realized that 20 million people around the world were surfing the Internet without using Microsoft software. As people and computers grew increasingly dependent on the Internet, Gates became concerned that Navigator or another Web browser could become a new communication standard and make Windows irrelevant.

Microsoft quickly purchased the rights to Spyglass, a browser program that had grown out of an early version of Mosaic. It used Spyglass as the basis for its own Web browser, called Internet Explorer, which it added to the Windows 95 operating system. Over the next year, Microsoft and Netscape raced to upgrade their browser programs, releasing improved versions every few months. Each company hoped that its latest innovations would enable it to establish the standard for the industry and take control of the growing market for Web browsers.

During these "browser wars," Microsoft employed a strategy of integrating its Internet Explorer Web browser more and more tightly with its Windows operating system. Since 90 percent of computers ran on Windows software, Internet Explorer was immediately the most widely distributed Web browser. Gates claimed that integrating the browser with Windows offered users the benefit of an "active desktop" that interacted seamlessly with the Web. But Netscape and other competitors—as well as many computer users—complained that such integration effectively forced people to use Explorer by making it very difficult to run Navigator or other non-Microsoft browsers through Windows. Netscape also claimed that Microsoft unfairly restricted competition by essentially giving away Explorer for free, since it was included within the operating system that was installed on nearly all new PCs. Sales of Navigator declined rapidly during this time, particularly after America Online (AOL)—

By 2001, when Microsoft Chairman Bill Gates unveiled the new Windows XP operating system, his company had risen to a dominant position in the market for Web browsers.

the largest online service provider in the United States—agreed to provide its customers with access to the Web using Microsoft's Internet Explorer browser.

In 1997 the U.S. Justice Department filed an antitrust lawsuit against Microsoft on behalf of Netscape and other competitors. The lawsuit, which made headlines throughout the late 1990s, charged that Microsoft had engaged in monopolistic practices in order to drive these companies out of business. Gates testified during the trial, providing a videotaped deposition that was played in court. Legal observers claimed that he seemed defiant and uncooperative, and some analysts said that his testimony was a turning point in the trial because it weakened Microsoft's credibility.

The trial concluded in June 2000, when Microsoft was found in violation of U.S. antitrust laws (this ruling came too late to save Netscape Communications from being acquired by America Online in 1999). The judge ordered the company to be broken up into two businesses—one centered

55

around the Windows operating system and the other focusing on Microsoft's software applications. Gates immediately condemned the ruling and launched a series of legal appeals. The appeals court upheld the ruling, but rejected the penalty and assigned the case to a new judge. In November 2001 Microsoft announced that it had reached a deal with the Justice Department to settle the case. Several states that had participated in the lawsuit criticized the deal, calling it a "slap on the wrist" for the company and noting that it enabled Microsoft to maintain its commanding position in the Web browser market. By this time, however, advancing technology had led to significant changes in browser software and reduced the importance of the lawsuit.

Chapter Five

THE "DOT.COM BOOM" GOES BUST

By the middle of 2000, it was possible to believe that we were all living in the Bizarro World, the Internet version of a parallel universe, in which everything, everything that was true at the beginning of the year, was reversed. None of the metrics that had been employed to evaluate the confounding Internet business were retained, and in a New York minute, the Internet suddenly became more than a little terrifying.

—John Motavalli, *Bamboozled at the Revolution*

Once the Internet had been opened up for commercial use, entrepreneurs responded by creating a wave of new businesses to exploit the technology. These online businesses became known as "dot.coms," after the three-letter domain abbreviation for commercial Web sites. As businesses rushed to establish a presence on the World Wide Web, investors quickly jumped on the Internet bandwagon, as well. Eager to discover the Internet start-up company that would become the "next big thing" and generate huge financial rewards, investors poured money into unproven Web-based businesses. "The dot.com success story … was fueled by a rush of investment money and hopes of revolutionary new business opportunities," Neil Munro wrote in the *National Journal*. "Investors saw each new company as a unique way to replicate the stock market success of Microsoft and other high-tech companies."

Throughout the late 1990s, dot.coms took in huge sums of money. This money came in the form of investments from venture capital firms—companies that provide funding for new business ventures, usually in exchange for a share of future profits as the new business grows. According to *Business Week,* the 6,000 high-tech and Internet start-up firms that launched during the 1990s attracted $100 billion in venture capital investments. Following the lead of Netscape Communications—the maker of the popular Navigator Web browser that had held a highly successful initial public stock offering (IPO) in 1995—about 450 of these fledgling Internet businesses sold shares on the stock market to become publicly owned companies. Internet stocks became a hot investment for professional and casual investors alike. "There were so many constituencies beating the drum for the IPO du jour that it was very difficult not to be convinced: Wall Street analysts, market researchers, venture capitalists, business school professors, and consultants," Clinton Wilder noted in *Information Week.* "And, of course, the media."

Dot.Coms Create a Booming Economy

The boom in investment in Internet start-ups contributed to a rapid rise in the overall value of the American stock markets. The NASDAQ stock exchange, with its emphasis on technology companies, rose by a remarkable 795 percent during the 1990s, closing at an all-time high of 5,048.62 points on March 13, 2000. Between the fourth quarter of 1999 and the first quarter of 2000, technology companies received an incredible $156 billion in investment capital (money realized from investors bidding up the price of shares on the stock market).

Many Web-based businesses saw their stock prices increase dramatically during the "dot.com boom" of the late 1990s. For example, shares of Yahoo!, maker of one of the Web's most popular search engines, traded at $30 each in 1998. By January 2000, the firm's stock price had increased to $250 per share, which made Yahoo! worth $133 billion—or more than General Motors and Ford Motor Company combined. Priceline.com, an online ticket-selling site that consistently lost money, at one point had a higher market value than the airlines whose seats it sold.

As the dot.coms accumulated huge amounts of investment capital, many of the firms began spending money at an amazing rate. Some high-tech start-ups built fancy corporate headquarters, complete with foosball tables, swimming pools, and masseuses. These companies believed such amenities would foster a casual working atmosphere in which creative and innovative thinking would thrive. Others took employees on expensive corporate retreats to Las

Yahoo! co-founders David Filo (left) and Jerry Yang (right).

Vegas or the Bahamas, or sponsored lavish parties for investors and members of the media.

Some analysts later noted that the dot.com spending frenzy reached its peak during the January 2000 Super Bowl. As the most-watched event on television, the Super Bowl always attracted high-profile advertisers willing to pay enormous fees to promote their products and services to a worldwide audience. The 2000 telecast featured commercials for a dozen fledgling Internet companies, each of which found enough cash to spend $2 million for a 30-second spot. Some of the best-remembered Super Bowl ads from that year featured a sock puppet representing the online pet-supply store Pets.com.

This cycle of massive investment in and spending by Web-based companies contributed to a record period of growth in the U.S. economy. Yet some experts warned that the dot.com boom was based on speculation rather than solid business principles. Traditional economic theories said that a firm's

"As we all know, the stock market was wrong. And its fall was more than just the bursting of the latest speculative bubble. No, this was a mass illusion of confusing the stock market with reality—not just in an investment sense, but in fundamental ways of thinking about what it means to build and grow a business."

stock price should reflect the level of its profits. In other words, companies that earned a higher level of profits on each dollar of investment they received should be worth more than those that earned less. In the case of Internet start-ups, however, the old rules did not seem to apply. Few of the start-ups were profitable during their early existence, and their extremely high market valuation was based instead on such new and unproven measures as revenue potential or number of visitors to a Web site.

Many Internet companies lacked a sensible business plan and failed to generate any earnings, yet investors still flocked to them. The feverish pursuit of Web-based profits not only led companies to disregard basic principles of business operation and planning, but also led investors to discount basic rules of investing. Even the most traditional stock brokers advised their clients not to miss out on the opportunity to "get rich quick" by investing in Internet stocks. Day-trading became a popular pastime, as people tried any means to make money from the rising stock market. The few analysts who criticized the boom, like investment expert Warren Buffett, were dismissed as "out of touch." "Healthy skepticism took a beating during the heady days of the dot.com run-up," Wilder acknowledged. "Those who questioned the 'inevitable' New Economy realities were called dinosaurs."

Nevertheless, a few economists stuck to their predictions that it was only a matter of time before the speculative bubble burst and the stock market returned to rationality. They claimed that the Internet investment boom was part of a natural process that followed any major technological advance. They pointed out that similar investment trends had occurred shortly after the introduction of such devices as telephones, radios, televisions, and personal computers, when innovators rushed to build businesses around the new technology. The first 25 years of the automobile industry, for example, saw the creation of more than 3,000 car manufacturers. A few of these companies succeeded in spectacular fashion, but most failed or were bought out by stronger competitors. Economists skeptical of the dot.com boom said that such a winnowing of competitors would inevitably occur among Internet businesses as well.

The Speculative Bubble Bursts

The dot.com bubble first showed signs of weakness on April 4, 2000. Microsoft, the world's most influential technology company, was then in the middle of a highly publicized court case. The U.S. Justice Department, acting on behalf of Netscape Communications and other competitors, had brought an antitrust lawsuit against Microsoft in 1997, charging that the software giant had engaged in monopolistic practices intended to drive its competition out of business. The suit claimed that Microsoft had unfairly restricted competition by integrating its Internet Explorer Web browser with its Windows operating system, which made it difficult for Windows users to choose alternative browser software. The case dragged on for more than two years.

Investment guru Warren Buffett was one of the few experts who warned that Internet stocks were overvalued during the dot.com boom.

A turning point came in early 2000, when Microsoft chairman Bill Gates testified in the court proceedings. Many observers felt that he appeared defiant and uncooperative, and it was generally agreed that his testimony significantly weakened the company's defense. Many experts said that Microsoft's best interests would be served by reaching a settlement out of court, rather than risking a judicial ruling that might break up the company. On April 4, however, the two sides announced that their efforts to reach a settlement had collapsed. Nervous about the impact a negative court ruling might have on the future of both Microsoft and the U.S. economy, investors began bailing out of the stock market as soon as they heard the news. The Dow Jones Industrial Average (an index of stock prices for some of the largest firms on the New York Stock Exchange) declined by 349.15 points, losing 7.64 percent of its value. It was the biggest one-day point drop in the history of the New York Stock Exchange.

In April 2000 the "dot.com" bubble burst and trading turned chaotic and desperate on market floors around the country, including this trading pit at the Chicago Mercantile Exchange.

The markets fluctuated widely over the next week or so, as uncertain investors tried to decide what to do. On April 11, several large technology firms—including Microsoft, Intel, Hewlett-Packard, and IBM—released earnings reports that did not meet investor expectations. As a result, the NASDAQ stock exchange suffered the second-largest drop in its history, falling 286.27 points. By the time the NASDAQ fell another 355.49 points on April 17, it was clear to many investors that the dot.com boom was over. Experts suddenly began looking at Internet companies in a new light and using time-tested measures to evaluate their investment potential. "Triggered by concerns about e-commerce profits, analysts like Merrill Lynch's Henry Blodget finally decided that P/E [price/earnings] ratios did matter when evaluating Internet companies," John Motavalli wrote in his book *Bamboozled at the Revolution.* "And once you adopted that approach, virtually all Internet companies started looking bad, because even the biggest, like Amazon, were losing lots of money."

Notorious Dot.Com Collapses

When the "dot.com" bubble burst in 2000, the Internet quickly became littered with the husks of numerous venture-driven, financially overvalued companies that fell victim to bankruptcy. Prominent examples of enterprises that were ruined by the market downturn included Kosmo.com, a New York-based online company that promised free one-hour delivery of small goods (clothing, books, office supplies, hot coffee, etc.); garden.com, which launched an ill-fated attempt to sell garden supplies over the Internet; and Webvan, a California-based online grocery business that collapsed under the weight of its own monstrous infrastructure expenditures.

The most infamous of the dot.com enterprises to fail, however, was probably pets.com. This company sought to make a big splash in the realm of pet supplies and accessories by pouring enormous sums of money into marketing and advertising. Much of this advertising was centered around its "spokesman," a sock puppet in the form of a dog. The pets.com dog even was featured in an extremely expensive commercial buy that appeared during the January 2000 Super Bowl. But the company, which received considerable financial aid from part-owner Amazon.com, never approached profitability, and its stock value plummeted during the early spring of 2001. In April 2001 pets.com declared bankruptcy, marking the end of one of the more memorable dot.com stories of the early Internet era.

Throughout the remainder of 2000, the news was full of stories about the disastrous collapse of the American stock market. Reporters who had once gushed over the latest dot.com millionaires now covered the "burn rates" at which Internet companies were going through their cash. Numerous Web-based businesses began laying off employees, closing down offices, and pulling advertisements in a desperate effort to reduce costs. It seemed as if a once-promising Internet company went out of business every day. The Dow Jones Internet Index, which measured the stock prices of key dot.com companies, declined by more than 72 percent between March and December 2000. Shares of such onetime stars as Priceline.com and eToys dropped by 99 percent from their highest levels.

The precipitous decline in the stock markets not only destroyed many Internet start-up businesses, but it also cost investors billions of dollars. A year after the crash, estimates of "paper" losses (the theoretical amount investors would lose if they purchased stocks at the highest price and sold at the lowest) ranged from $500 billion to $2 trillion. As a result, the dot.com collapse sparked a recession that spread throughout the American economy. It also led to increased scrutiny of corporate business practices, as well as government investigations of some Internet bankers and analysts. "As we all know, the stock market was wrong. And its fall was more than just the bursting of the latest speculative bubble," Wilder stated. "No, this was a mass illusion of confusing the stock market with reality—not just in an investment sense, but in fundamental ways of thinking about what it means to build and grow a business."

Lessons from the Rise and Fall of the Dot.Coms

Immediately after the dot.com bubble burst, media coverage focused on the event's negative impact on employees, investors, and the overall economy. Within a year, however, some analysts began to notice that the rise and fall of the dot.coms seemed to offer valuable lessons for both entrepreneurs and investors. In addition, they pointed out that despite the financial woes afflicting many Internet-based enterprises, the Internet continued to hold the potential to transform American business. "The current sense of despair in the dot.com universe may be as overdone as last year's euphoria," stated a December 2000 *New York Times* editorial. "The Internet, after all, really is a transforming technology that has revolutionized the way we communicate. What recent months suggest, however, is that it may not be an indiscriminate, magical new means of making money."

The reassessment of the dot.com bust began during the 2000 holiday season, when it became clear that the public was by no means ready to give up on the Internet. "As it turns out, many consumers and businesses never mistook the overinflated Internet stocks for the underlying value of the Internet," Timothy J. Mullaney wrote in *Business Week*. "They kept going online, and didn't pull back just because Amazon.com's shares dropped or the fallen highflier Webvan Group Inc. stopped delivering groceries." In fact, the amount consumers spent shopping online in 2000 was two-thirds higher than in 1999, at the height of the dot.com boom. And the total continued to increase over the next few years, not only in the United States but around the world.

The initial success of the dot.coms attracted many traditional retailers, like Wal-Mart, to the Internet. Once the boom ended, the online sales of these retailers surpassed those of pure Internet companies for the first time. In the meantime, though, the Web-based businesses that survived the crash increased their competitiveness. Analysts soon noticed that both online and traditional businesses were using the Internet to increase productivity through more accurate sales forecasts, lower inventories, and improved communication with suppliers. "To the surprise of many, the Net is actually delivering on many of its supposedly discredited promises," Mullaney noted. "The Internet is connecting farflung people and businesses more tightly than ever. It is helping companies slash costs. It is speeding the pace of innovation and jacking up productivity. And even some of those harebrained business models are working."

After the stock market crash, venture capital firms and investors approached high-tech and Internet businesses with extreme caution. Before, they had thrown money at anyone with a new idea. Now, they returned to basic principles like profit percentages and margins on sales to evaluate the investment value of companies. This cautious approach ensured that most new Internet start-ups possessed solid business plans that emphasized profitability over market share.

Partly as a result of the lessons learned from the dot.com bust, commercial use of the Internet took off in about 2003. Consumer online spending reached $95 billion that year, while business-to-business e-commerce was an impressive $2.4 trillion. Furthermore, some experts predicted that the Internet's impact on business would experience even more robust growth as the technology matured. "The journey, after all, is just beginning," Mullaney wrote in 2003. "At eight years, the Web is the same age color TV was when it turned profitable in 1962. And when color sets really got TV rolling, we all know what happened: New industries sprouted from it that were a complete and utter surprise [like advertising and cable television].... No doubt e-business has many more surprises in store."

Chapter Six

THE SOCIETAL IMPACT
OF THE INTERNET

⊷⊸⊷⊸

> We are watching something historic happen, and it will affect the world seismically, rocking us the same way the discovery of the scientific method, the invention of printing, and the arrival of the Industrial Age did.
>
> —Bill Gates, *The Road Ahead*

The development and worldwide growth of the Internet has had far-reaching effects on human society. The vast computer network and the information resources it contains have led to important changes in the realms of politics, business, education, entertainment, and communication. "The Web has sent a jolt through our culture, zapping our economy, our ideas about sharing creative works, and possibly even institutions such as religion and government," David Weinberger wrote in *Small Pieces Loosely Joined.*

In many ways, the Internet has connected people like no previous technology, tearing down boundaries to create a global village. "Through the dot-com bubble and bust, one trend has never wavered," Olga Kharif noted in *Business Week Online.* "Every year, millions more people around the world are using the Internet to interact in more ways than ever before—to date, find old classmates, check on medical ailments and cures, to read and express alternative views of the news, and even to get live sales help online."

The Internet has quickly become integrated into many elements of modern life—but not without controversy. For example, while the Internet undoubtedly provides convenience and enjoyment for those with easy access to it, some analysts warn that the rapid proliferation of the technology has

Students in Durham, North Carolina, share laptops from the school's mobile computer lab for a class project.

created a "digital divide" separating regular Internet users from those who lack technical training and access. Since this divide generally breaks along racial and socioeconomic lines, critics worry that the rise of Internet technology is reinforcing and deepening rifts between various segments of American society—and making it even harder for poor minority and white families to escape their impoverished circumstances.

Critics also point out that the open exchange of information and ideas made possible by the Internet has left users vulnerable to new types of crime, commonly dubbed "cybercrime." These unlawful activities include identity theft, fraud, copyright infringement, cyberterrorism, child pornography, and harassment. Finally, concerns have been voiced that the Internet—despite its wide assortment of wonderful tools for exploring, understanding, and interacting with people all around the world—has actually led some users to become isolated in the world of cyberspace rather than maintain healthy relations with friends, family, and the larger community in which they live.

Origins of the "Netsurfing" Metaphor

Jean Armour Polly

In June 1992 the *Wilson Library Bulletin,* a periodical for librarians, published an article by New York state librarian Jean Armour Polly that explained the basics of the rapidly growing Internet in layman's terms. The article was also made available on the Internet for downloading in December 1992 (see "A Librarian Shares the Joy of 'Surfing' the Internet," p. 170). One of the first articles of its kind to appear in the mainstream media, it effectively captured the growing sense that an exciting new tool for researching and exploring the world was coming into being.

Polly's article, "Surfing the Internet: An Introduction," placed an enduring metaphor for Internet exploration into the American lexicon. After its appearance, the image of users "surfing" the Internet for knowledge and recreation became ingrained not only in the minds of people dedicated to this emerging technology, but also in the imaginations of people making their first tentative forays onto the Internet.

Looking back on the creation of her influential article, Polly confirmed that she wanted a memorable metaphor for Internet exploration. "I wanted something that expressed the fun I had using the Internet, as well as hit on the skill, and yes, endurance necessary to use it well," she wrote in "Birth of a Metaphor," available on her Web site http://www.netmom.com. "I also needed something that would evoke a sense of randomness, chaos, and even danger." But she was unable to settle on a satisfactory metaphor until she took note of her mouse pad, which portrayed a surfer negotiating a big wave, with the words "Information Surfer" emblazoned across the top. From there it was just a short leap for her to coin the phrase "surfing the Internet," and today, millions of Internet users continue to refer to their online activities as "surfing."

The Digital Divide

Beginning with the introduction of the World Wide Web in the early 1990s, Internet use has increased rapidly. The network connected 3 million people around the world in 1993. This total increased to 38 million in 1994, reached 130 million in 1998, and topped 300 million in 2000. By 2004, an estimated 800 million people around the world had access to the Internet, including 207 million in the United States. Surveys conducted for the Pew Internet and American Life Project in 2003 indicated that Internet users comprised 63 percent of the adult population of the United States. Among these "online Americans," 88 percent said that the Internet played a role in their daily lives, and 64 percent said that a loss of Internet access would affect their daily routines.

Access to this technology has long been held disproportionately by affluent white Americans, however. This state of affairs first came to public attention in 1999, when the U.S. Department of Commerce issued a famous study called *Falling Through the Net: Defining the Digital Divide.* The study found that U.S. households with annual incomes of $75,000 or higher were 20 times more likely to have access to the Internet than households with the lowest annual income levels. It also showed that white American families were 2.5 times more likely to have Internet access at home than African-American and Hispanic families. These statistics triggered widespread calls for the development of new policy reforms and educational programs to close this gap.

In 2002 the Department of Commerce released a study called *A Nation Online: How Americans Are Expanding Their Use of the Internet.* This study showed progress in addressing the "digital divide," with Internet usage rising rapidly among the poor and minority citizens. Nonetheless, their access to the Internet continued to lag behind that of middle-class and affluent white citizens. The results indicated that families with annual incomes less than $15,000 increased their Internet usage from 9.2 percent in 1997 to 25 percent in 2001 (a 63 percent increase). Meanwhile, usage among families with incomes over $75,000 increased from 44.5 percent to 78.9 percent during this period (a 44 percent increase). Usage among African-American families increased from 13.2 percent in 1997 to 39.8 percent in 2001 (a 67 percent increase), but usage among white families went from 25.3 percent to 59.9 percent (a 58 percent increase) during the same period.

Continued inequities in access to the Internet—and the educational and economic benefits contained therein—are a source of great concern to many

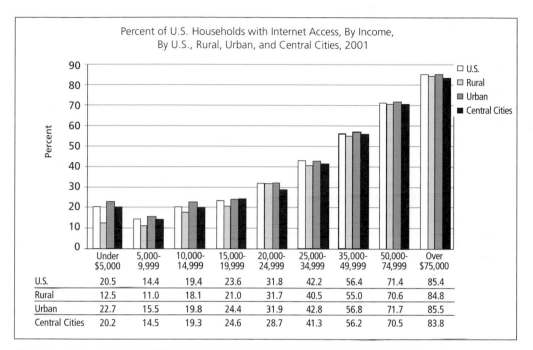

Percent of U.S. Households with Internet Access, By Income, By U.S., Rural, Urban, and Central Cities, 2001

	Under $5,000	5,000-9,999	10,000-14,999	15,000-19,999	20,000-24,999	25,000-34,999	35,000-49,999	50,000-74,999	Over $75,000
U.S.	20.5	14.4	19.4	23.6	31.8	42.2	56.4	71.4	85.4
Rural	12.5	11.0	18.1	21.0	31.7	40.5	55.0	70.6	84.8
Urban	22.7	15.5	19.8	24.4	31.9	42.8	56.8	71.7	85.5
Central Cities	20.2	14.5	19.3	24.6	28.7	41.3	56.2	70.5	83.8

Source: NTIA and ESA, U.S. Department of Commerce, using U.S. Bureau of the Census Current Population Survey Supplements

analysts. They fear that people without the training or financial resources to utilize the Internet will be increasingly pushed to the margins of American society. Indeed, these analysts express concern that unequal access will eventually create a two-tiered society of Internet users and non-users. And they predict that in the future, non-users will face even more significant disadvantages in education, in the work force, and in other aspects of daily life, as society become progressively more dependent on the Internet and other forms of information technology.

The Global Village

The Internet has made it faster, easier, and less expensive for people located in distant parts of the world to communicate with each other. By helping users learn about other cultures and interact with people of different nationalities, the Internet has created an online community where many people feel like global citizens. Supporters claim that the Internet serves to break down boundaries between people—and not only geographic boundaries, but

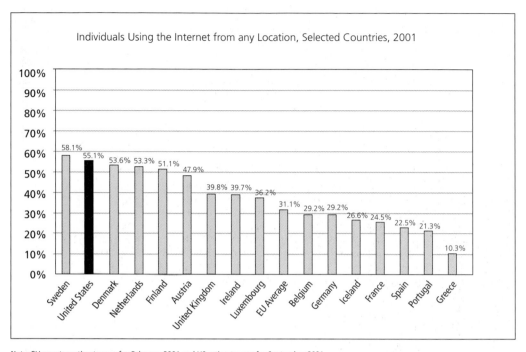

Individuals Using the Internet from any Location, Selected Countries, 2001

Note: EU country estimates are for February 2001 and US estimates are for September 2001.
Source: European Union, http://europa.eu.int/information_society/eeurope/index_en.htm and U.S. Department of Commerce, Economic and Statistics Administration.

also barriers relating to age, gender, social class, race, and religion. But critics see a growing "digital divide" here as well—between citizens of developed nations, where Internet access is widespread, and those of developing nations, where the technology has been slow to penetrate. People in poorer countries could certainly benefit from using the Internet to gain information about health, hygiene, child care, agriculture, and other issues. Yet the poor telecommunications infrastructure and limited financial resources of these countries severely limit access.

One way in which the Internet has helped to create a global village is by making international news and information readily available to users around the world. This is seen as a possible force for change in countries with repressive governments. In many cases, repressive governments have found it more difficult to restrict citizens' access to such information online than when it was delivered through newspapers, television, or radio—all of which could be controlled or censored by the state. Not all citizens of the world have equal access to the Internet, however. Some countries like China and Saudi Arabia limit access to govern-

An Iranian college student visits a Tehran Internet café to conduct research for a school project.

ment-approved Web sites, though some citizens can still get information about current events through international e-mail contacts. In other countries, like Burma and Malaysia, government authorities track citizens' Internet usage close-ly, and in North Korea accessing the Internet is actually a criminal offense.

Where Internet access is available, information is largely free from politi-cal control. In these nations, citizens are exposed to news and ideas from the outside world. Some analysts believe that the knowledge and awareness gained from Internet resources could force repressive regimes to make mean-ingful reforms or risk popular unrest, which could destabilize their govern-ments. "The presence of advanced communications systems promises to make nations more alike and reduce the importance of national boundaries," Bill Gates wrote in *The Road Ahead*. "Commercial satellite broadcasts to nations such as China and Iran offer citizens glimpses of the outside world that are not necessarily sanctioned by their governments. This new access to information can draw people together by increasing their understanding of other cultures."

Some social scientists, however, have expressed concerns about the global reach of the Internet. Currently, Internet content primarily reflects Western culture and values. Social scientists worry that as Internet content filters to all corners of the globe, it may have the unintended effect of homogenizing distinct societies and reducing cultural diversity. Critics point out, for example, that the Internet encourages users to communicate in English, which is the most prevalent language on the network. These critics express concern that the Internet's emphasis on worldwide communication standards might eventually drive rare languages out of existence. On the other hand, some experts claim that the Internet might actually help save rare languages by encouraging their use in Internet chat rooms and discussion groups.

The Internet and the Political Process

Even in democratic nations, the Internet has played an increasingly important role in the political process. It helps political activists to organize demonstrations and promote their views, for example, and its electronic mail feature provides an efficient and convenient means for concerned citizens to communicate with their representatives. The Internet also facilitates voter registration, and the future may see more electronic elections. Internet voting was first used in the United States during the Arizona Democratic primary in 2000, when over half of all voters cast their ballots online. Since that time, numerous states have constructed electronic registration and voting mechanisms for their citizens.

Proponents say that as electronic elections become more commonplace, they will increase voter turnout and make the process of counting ballots quicker and more accurate. But other analysts insist that Internet voting will not be a fair and feasible option until universal access is achieved. They fear that an Internet-based voting process will be inherently unfair until people who are socioeconomically disadvantaged enjoy the same level of access to the Internet as financially secure white citizens.

In recent years, the Internet has been widely adopted as a medium for political advertising and campaign fundraising. Former Vermont Governor Howard Dean demonstrated the value of the Internet for fundraising during his bid for the 2004 Democratic presidential nomination. Although Dean did not win the nomination, he waged a highly successful Internet operation that raised millions of dollars and attracted millions of voters to his campaign for the presidency. Other candidates quickly adopted the Internet as well, establishing campaign Web sites and using e-mail to reach target audiences. *InternetWeek* reported that spending for political advertising on the Internet exceeded $25 million in 2004, an increase of over 850 percent from 2000.

The Virtual Classroom

In the United States, an entire generation of children is coming of age with the Internet as an integral part of their daily lives. A 2004 study by the Kaiser Family Foundation found that around 60 percent of American kids between the ages of 8 and 18 used the Internet on a typical day. Thanks to a variety of public programs and private initiatives, fully 99 percent of American schools offered Internet access to their students. A majority of school-age children were also connected at home, although the numbers varied based on racial and economic factors. For example, the study indicated that 80 percent of white children had home Internet access, compared to 61 percent of African-American children and 67 percent of Hispanic children.

The Internet has a wide variety of applications for education. Students can use it to communicate with teachers and classmates through e-mail or instant messaging. The Internet facilitates "distance learning," which enables students in remote locations to attend classes from their homes. Students can also submit assignments via e-mail when they are home sick or away on vacation. Other possible student uses of the Internet include accessing online study aids; making virtual visits to museums, art galleries, libraries, and historic sites; obtaining information about colleges and careers; and keeping track of course schedules, homework assignments, and extracurricular activities (see "Bill Gates Discusses the Internet's Potential Impact on Education," p. 177).

One of the most important educational applications of the Internet is its use as a research tool for homework and school projects. Indeed, the Internet has transformed the process of doing research, as students today routinely start with online resources. Many research materials can now be found online, giving students access to a broad range of information. Online databases containing periodical articles, for example, offer far more comprehensive resources than what might be available to those students through local

75

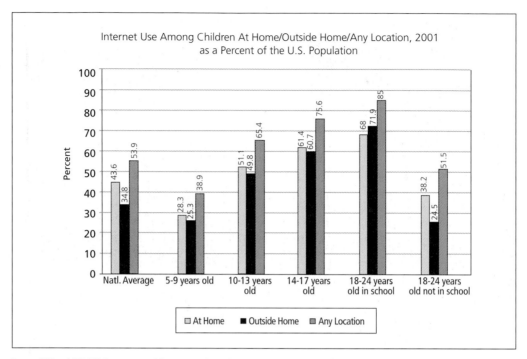

Internet Use Among Children At Home/Outside Home/Any Location, 2001 as a Percent of the U.S. Population

Source: NTIA and ESA, U.S. Department of Commerce, using U.S. Census Bureau Current Population Survey Supplements

libraries. Search engines can be used to guide students to additional online materials from businesses, non-profit groups, educational institutions, news organizations, and other authoritative sources.

Supporters of expanding the Internet's role in education claim that the technology helps create active learners who take responsibility for their own work. They also say that distance learning could help address teacher shortages and declining school-district budgets, while also offering broader educational opportunities. Critics, however, argue that excessive reliance on the Internet for education causes students to miss out on important social interactions. They also point out that the Web contains a great deal of unreliable information. For some students, turning to an Internet search engine has become the first—or even the only—step in the research process. This has led to concerns about students' use of erroneous information and their ability to determine which sites are accurate and authoritative. Since there is no guarantee of the accuracy of information on the Web, evaluating information sources and thinking critically have become even more important. And the ease of plagiarism—since students

An elementary school student in Newport News, Virginia, surfs the Web on a school computer.

could simply cut and paste information from electronic sources or even use the Web to purchase a whole research paper—has led many experienced teachers to scrutinize students' homework for signs of copying. But in some cases, teachers can provide little guidance to Internet-savvy students raised since birth in an increasingly technology-driven environment.

The Internet Business Revolution

The Internet has fundamentally altered the world of business as well. It has introduced widespread changes in the relationships between companies and their customers, suppliers, and employees, resulting in improved customer service, reduced inventories, and increased productivity. One of the most significant impacts of the Internet has been in facilitating communication between businesses and their customers. Web sites allow businesses to maintain constant contact with customers, collect information about the use of their products, and respond to customer feedback and changing customer

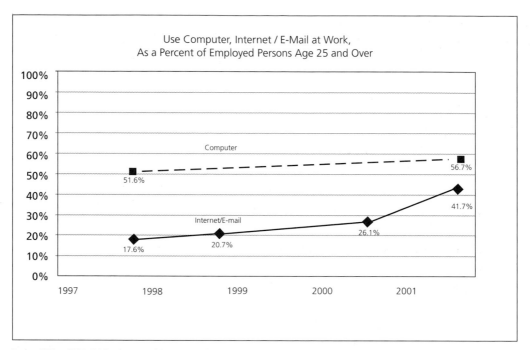

Use Computer, Internet / E-Mail at Work,
As a Percent of Employed Persons Age 25 and Over

Source: NTIA and ESA, U.S. Department of Commerce, using U.S. Census Bureau Current Population Survey Supplements

needs in a more efficient and timely manner than ever before. Similarly, businesses can connect their computer systems with those of suppliers, creating a feedback loop that improves product design and quality and eliminates the need to carry large inventories.

The Internet has also contributed to fundamental changes in the relationship between employer and employee. For instance, the technology has made possible a "virtual office," which allows employees in various physical locations to work together. In fact, the Internet allows people to work almost anywhere, provided they have access to a portable computer and a mobile phone. Numerous people around the world have seized on this new reality. Instead of toiling in a conventional office environment, greater numbers of people than ever before are working at home or in other remote locations, using the Internet as a communication link to their employers. These remote work locations are made possible by e-mail, which has emerged as perhaps the single most important element of modern business communications.

By allowing people in distant locations to communicate and collaborate, the Internet helps large companies with offices all over the world operate

Taxes and the Internet

Some analysts claim that Web-based businesses enjoy an unfair advantage over traditional retailers because they do not require customers to pay sales tax on purchases. They are thus able to offer prices that are more attractive to would-be buyers than those posted by traditional "brick and mortar" enterprises. Consumers are supposed to pay any sales tax due from Internet purchases on their own, but this rarely occurs. Most consumers are either not aware that the tax is owed or ignore the regulations in order to save themselves money.

Some state and local governments are eager to enforce tax laws on Internet commerce, both to protect traditional businesses and to raise revenues for schools, roads, police departments, and other public services. But online merchants argue that requiring them to comply with sales tax laws from 46 states and thousands of local governments would place an unfair burden on their businesses.

more efficiently. Small businesses stand to benefit from the Internet in many ways, as well. For example, several small businesses that possess different skills could work together to form a "virtual business" and compete against larger companies. The Internet also helps small businesses compete on more equal terms by giving them access to customers all over the world.

Finally, the Internet has prompted the creation of entirely new types of businesses—and has been cited as the chief culprit in the demise or decline of various traditional fields of business. For example, online travel sites now give customers access to the same airline and hotel reservation systems used by travel agents. The popularity of these sites has devastated many traditional travel agencies that handled travel bookings for clients in the pre-Internet era. In 2003 alone, for example, the number of travel agencies operating in the United States declined by an estimated 13 percent.

Other industries also have suffered downtowns that have been attributed, at least in part, to the unparalleled power of the Internet. The recording industry, for example, suffered a 15 percent decrease in CD sales in 2001 and 2002, as Internet users downloaded billions of digital songs.

As consumer spending on the Internet approached $100 billion in 2003, experts continue to debate the overall impact of electronic commerce. They note that although shopping on the Internet offers convenience and access to a wide selection of merchandise, a significant proportion of consumers (mostly older people) remain resistant to it. Some of these skeptics worry that it is not safe to provide credit card numbers online, while others simply prefer to see and touch products before buying them. Nonetheless, Internet commerce is expected to claim a steadily greater share of total business in the years ahead, as anti-fraud measures are strengthened, online advertising becomes more sophisticated, and today's children and adolescents—raised in a world where Web surfing is as familiar as bicycle riding—reach adulthood and become America's dominant consumers.

The Internet and Communications

The Internet has revolutionized communication in modern life. One of the most prevalent Internet formats for communications is e-mail, which is now an integral part of Americans' daily life. E-mail is fast, cheap, and easy to use, which has made it the primary form of communication for many people. In the work place, it provides a quick and affordable way to keep in touch with employees and include them in group discussions, and it creates a written record of agreements. It allows business people to send short messages that can be read later, when the recipient is available; to share documents; to avoid lengthy phone calls or meetings; and to collaborate on projects. In the home, e-mail is easy to use and inexpensive, allowing far-flung family and friends to keep in touch.

Yet even devoted e-mail users are quick to point out its problems. E-mail may make communication less personal and may discourage face-to-face contact. In some cases, e-mail can create misunderstandings, since brief messages tend to be abrupt and since nonverbal cues like body language and facial expressions are lost in electronic communication. In the future, however, the introduction of video technology like Webcams could help eliminate such problems. And while e-mail can save time, it can also be a major time-waster. The speed of communication creates its own problems. While it is an incredible asset, it often leaves people feeling that they must respond immediately to every note, contributing to the sense or urgency that is so prevalent in American life today. And in the business world, the pervasiveness of e-mail access can also lead workers to feel that they are always "on" and that they should always be available to their employers, even when at home or on vacation.

Another major drawback to e-mail is junk e-mail, or spam, which marketers use to promote their products. Opening e-mail often includes spending valuable time sorting through and deleting these junk messages. Filtering technologies have been developed to block it, and legislation such as the CAN-SPAM (Controlling the Assault of Non-Solicited Pornography and Marketing) Act of 2003 has been passed to destroy it, but still spam continues to be a major problem for Internet users, at home and at work.

Despite such inconveniences, few people would choose to live without e-mail. Indeed, these 1999 comments from Andrew Leonard in *Newsweek* still ring true today:

> If we accept that the creation of the globe-spanning Internet is one of the most important technological innovations of the last half of this century, then we much give e-mail—the living embodiment of human connection across the Net—pride of place. The way we interact with each other is changing; e-mail is both the catalyst and the instrument of that change. The scope of the phenomenon is mind-boggling.... Forget about the Web or e-commerce or even online pornography: e-mail is the Internet's true killer app—the software application that we simply must have.

While e-mail is fast becoming ubiquitous in American society, other forms of Internet communication are important as well. Two of the most common are Internet Relay Chat (IRC) and instant messaging (IM). In IRC, people are able to communicate in real time with people from all over the world. There are various separate networks of IRC servers. An individual can connect to an IRC server and choose one or more "channels" to join a conversation. These conversations can be public, where the messages can be read by everyone on the channel, or private, where the messages are sent between two people. By contrast, IM chat refers to a range of applications that offer real-time one-on-one text messaging services over the Internet, as well as such services as sharing photos, music files, and video. IM includes a small window on the computer desktop that allows users to send messages to a list of personal contacts. That list, called the "Buddy List," is a special feature of the IM software that allows users to see who among their friends is online at the same time.

According to the 2004 Pew Internet and American Life Project, more than 53 million American adults use IM, particularly young adults and technology enthusiasts. That represents 42 percent of Internet users, and the numbers are growing. IM is becoming more prevalent in the business world, where 11 million American adults use IM at work. Many of these business users feel that IM improves their productivity, but some feel that it encourages jokes, gossip, rumors, and other distractions. Not surprisingly, there are great differences in IM use among different age groups, with those who are younger using IM more frequently than older people. Teenagers, for example, are perhaps the most dedicated IM users.

Many analysts see the value of IM continuing to grow in the coming years, with younger users leading the way. Stephen Abram, librarian and president of the Canadian Library Association, explained why people should adopt IM: "E-mail is just sending letters and memos faster than our grandparents did. IM is having electronic conversations—it's the text version of a phone call—not a letter…. I believe that, in the end, IM will transform our culture and behavior, just like phones and e-mail did…. Our [student] users are entering a new world where the tools of commerce and work will have adapted to them—instead of the world many of us lived through where we, of necessity, had to adapt to rapidly changing tools. There is likely no single job or profession that will not be affected by ever more powerful IM systems integrated directly into their workplace applications and environment."

Criminal Activity and Other Dangers of the Internet

For all of the positive contributions the Internet has made to society, it has also produced a number of drawbacks, including criminal activity, sexually explicit material, and invasion of privacy. In fact, many non-users avoid the Internet because they are afraid they will fall victim to online scams or identity theft. Some analysts bemoan the evolution of Internet content toward intrusive advertising and pornography. "The Internet passed through challenges like the 1988 worm, viruses, the Y2K crisis, the dot.com collapse, and the terrorists' attacks of September 11, 2001, with hardly a hiccup. It is based on a robust design," Paul E. Ceruzzi wrote in *A History of Modern Computing*. "As for the content and quality of information that the Internet conveys,

American soldiers based near Fallujah, Iraq, visit cyberspace via a military-style Internet café.

however, it has indeed been tragic [watching it evolve] into a stream of information polluted with pop-up ads, spam, and pornography."

The Internet enables criminals to target larger numbers of victims more quickly and at greater distances than ever before. Cybercriminals take many forms, from hackers who break into computer systems to steal information to sexual predators who prowl chat rooms for potential victims. Another type of Internet criminal is the vandal who creates and distributes harmful programs known as viruses, which can destroy data and disable computers. One of the most common sources of viruses are files attached to e-mail messages. Some attached files contain malicious programs that automatically send copies of themselves to everyone on an infected computer's e-mail address list. The first virus of this type, called Melissa, caused $80 million in damage when it was released in 1999.

In fact, viruses can be so effective in shutting down computer systems that some governments are developing them to use as weapons in wartime. Taiwan, for example, has long been locked in a bitter struggle over independence with

China, which claims the island nation as part of its territory. Fearful of an invasion from Chinese military forces, Taiwanese leaders have stockpiled an arsenal of 1,000 viruses to unleash against Chinese computer systems. This view of the computer virus—as a deterrent against attack or weapon of war—has become integral to national defense strategies all around the globe.

The growth of the Internet has been accompanied by an increase in online fraud. Criminals have developed a wide range of e-mail scams designed to trick unsuspecting people into revealing such personal information as bank account numbers. They have also established "packet sniffing" software to steal credit card numbers and other sensitive information that is sent via e-mail. Some sophisticated criminals collect Social Security numbers and use them to pillage people's financial resources, ruining their credit in the process.

Many people express particular concerns about the dangers the Internet poses for children. These threats range from pornographic, violent, and racist material on the World Wide Web to sexual predators who attempt to contact minors through chat rooms and other Internet forums. Parental control features on Web browsers and e-mail filters are only marginally effective in preventing young people from encountering such material. Law enforcement task forces—though they have made numerous arrests of sexual predators through Internet stings—are unable to identify all users who enter chat rooms for illegal purposes.

Although many people agree with the need to prevent children from accessing violent, racist, and pornographic material on the Internet, some worry that the methods commonly used to protect children from inappropriate content lead to censorship of the Web. For example, the software programs used to filter Web content in schools and libraries sometimes prohibit access to legitimate topics, like breast cancer. While restricting users' access to Web content is difficult, regulating the creation and posting of content is nearly impossible. "Regulation has traditionally distinguished between public and private communication. You can say things at home you would never broadcast on the air," George Conrades of GTE explained in *Vital Speeches of the Day*. "But the Internet is both private, in the form of e-mail … and public, in the case of Web sites and chat groups." Since no one government controls the Web, sites that contain material that is illegal in certain countries can simply make the material available through Web servers located in different countries. Efforts to hold Internet Service Providers (ISPs) responsible for the content on their servers have thus far been ineffective, because the content is so difficult to control.

Critics of censorship also argue that people should be able to express any views they wish on the Web. These free speech advocates admit that some Internet content is disturbing and obscene. But they say that regulating Internet content is contrary to the principles of free and democratic societies, including the United States, which guarantees freedom of speech in the First Amendment to the Constitution. These critics worry that government restrictions on Internet content and operations will smother the Internet before it reaches its full potential as an agent of social change. One such critic was John Perry Barlow, a co-founder of the Electronic Frontier Project and faculty member at Harvard Law School who wrote an influential essay in 1996 opposing censorship on the Internet (see "John Perry Barlow's 'Declaration of Independence for Cyberspace,'" p. 174).

Internet users are the perpetrators of another type of online criminal activity: copyright infringement. Text, photographs, sounds, and videos are easily converted into digital form and distributed across the Internet. Oftentimes these materials are the intellectual property of individuals or companies and are protected by copyright. It is illegal to download and use copyrighted material without permission from its owner. But many Internet users choose to ignore the law, downloading millions of copyrighted software programs, songs, videos, and images every day. "Somewhere along the line, Americans—indeed, computer users everywhere—have made a collective decision that since no one can make us pay for entertainment, we're not going to," Lev Grossman wrote in *Time* magazine. The software industry loses billions of dollars in sales each year as a result of people making illegal copies of programs. Movies and music albums routinely appear online before they are officially released in theaters or record stores. According to *Time*, 2.6 billion music files were downloaded illegally every month in 2003. This situation became very costly to record companies, which reacted to declining sales by taking legal action against file-sharing services like Napster as well as against individuals who downloaded copyrighted music files. Such lawsuits generated a great deal of media attention and raised awareness of the potential penalties for illegal downloading. As more people became aware of the illegality of their actions, the trend showed signs of slowing. Some experts pointed to the growing popularity of subscription and pay-per-song services, like Apple's I-Tunes, as evidence that Internet users were becoming more respectful of copyright protection.

Despite its many problems, however, the Internet still offers tremendous benefits to society. "If the information highway is able to increase the understanding citizens of one country have about their neighboring countries, and thereby reduce international tensions, that, in and of itself, could be sufficient to justify the cost of implementation," Bill Gates noted in *The Road Ahead*. "If it was used only by scientists, permitting them to collaborate more effectively and to find cures for the still-incurable diseases, that alone would be invaluable. If the system was only for kids, so that they could pursue their interests in and out of the classroom, that by itself would transform the human condition. The information highway won't solve every problem, but it will be a positive force in many areas."

Internet Privacy

Privacy issues associated with the Internet have taken center stage in recent years. Many Web sites track visitors digitally and keep a record of their purchases. Critics object to this information gathering as an invasion of privacy. They contend that such information could be used by businesses to target advertising, or by governments to compile profiles of individuals' political views, health status, sexual orientation, and other personal information. Defenders of these information-gathering practices assert that the collection of personal information enables Web sites to customize visitors' experience.

Government oversight of individuals' activities on the Internet has also increased markedly since the mid-1990s, when the World Wide Web first exploded into prominence. The most high-profile battles over Internet privacy rights have been waged since the 2001 passage of the Patriot Act. This piece of legislation, passed by Congress following the terrorist attacks against the United States on September 11, 2001, gave the federal government broad powers to investigate the activities of suspected terrorists—including new authority to track Internet usage by individuals.

Defenders of these and other measures contained in the Patriot Act characterize them as valuable tools in the fight against terrorism, and they insist that they do not erode the basic freedoms and liberties enjoyed by Americans. Detractors charge that various elements of the Patriot Act, including those providing for the surveillance of the Internet activities of people not formally charged with wrongdoing, are an outrageous violation of the right to privacy and an unacceptable flouting of basic Constitutional rights.

The Internet and the Community Commons

Many observers acknowledge the beneficial effect the Internet *can* have on the understanding and appreciation of other cultures and perspectives. But they also express concern that the new technology is actually breeding a new era of isolationism in society, both in the United States and elsewhere. These critics contend that too many Internet users are retreating from the "community commons"—real-life environments in which the free and open exchange of ideas, information, and perspectives is encouraged. Instead, they're spending time on Web sites that provide comfortable affirmations of already-entrenched belief systems. Analysts express concern that this trend is fueling a new era of division and polarization in society.

The Internet has certainly had the beneficial effect of creating new connections among people and increasing human knowledge and understanding. But excessive time spent online has been cited as a major culprit in the increasing prevalence of social isolation in modern society. "What good does it do our society to take us away from a close, physical community and put us in touch with distant strangers?" Clifford Stoll declared in *Silicon Snake Oil.* "The things people yearn for most—a community, a relationship with commitment and trust—are exactly what you don't have online."

The mesmerizing effect that the Internet can have on some children and adolescents has attracted particular concern from educators, parents, and sociologists. They acknowledge that surfing the Web, playing online games, and communicating electronically with their peers can help young people develop skill sets that will serve them well in adulthood. But they warn that excessive time spent on the Internet can—like excessive television watching—stunt the development of critical social skills, reduce their availability for family interaction, and have a negative impact on physical health and well-being.

Chapter Seven

THE FUTURE
OF THE INTERNET

The entire computer revolution, including the Internet, hasn't begun yet. We're not in the middle of it—we're at the dawn of it. It's like trying to comprehend the magnitude of the oceans if all you've done is stand on the beach watching the waves breaking.

—Bran Ferren, *Discover* magazine

In the years immediately following the collapse of the dot.com economy, some analysts claimed that the Internet's period of rapid growth and development had come to an end. Few successful new Web-based businesses emerged during this time—the Google search engine being a notable exception—so many experts predicted that the technology boom had reached a plateau. But others argued that the hundreds of millions of Internet users around the world were developing exciting new applications for the technology every day. While admitting that no one knew for certain what the future might hold, they claimed that the Internet revolution had only just begun.

"Each transformation [of the computer] was accompanied by assertions that further transformations were unlikely, yet each time someone managed to break through," Paul E. Ceruzzi wrote in *A History of Modern Computing*. "The latest transformation, to the World Wide Web, was also preceded by statements that the computer industry was stagnating, that there was, to paraphrase a software salesman, 'no more low-hanging fruit.' He was wrong, and those who predict that the World Wide Web is the ultimate resting place for computing will no doubt be wrong as well."

Some observers believe that it is only a matter of time before people begin building large numbers of successful Web-based businesses again. Marc Andreessen, creator of the revolutionary Mosaic Web browser and founder of Netscape Communications, argued in 2004 that economic conditions were ripe for a new wave of technological development. "If you launch an Internet business today, it's probably going to cost you about a tenth of what it would have cost five years ago, but you're going to have 10 times more consumers you can address and probably 10 times the ad revenue," he told *USA Today.* "And people are going to be 10 times more willing to buy online. So you have this big economic swing."

In contemplating the future, many experts predict that the Internet will be increasingly combined with such emerging technologies as wireless connections, global positioning systems (GPS), and radio-frequency identification (RFID). They believe that the integration of these technologies will help transform the Internet from a communications medium into the center of an ever-expanding universe of Web-enabled electronic devices—ranging from cellular telephones, personal digital assistants (PDAs), and handheld computers to automobiles and home appliances—that will allow people to interact with the network anytime, anywhere.

"The coming wave doesn't even have a name yet," wrote Kevin Maney in *USA Today.* "Some in tech call it the world network. A big part of the promise is that it will turn the Web around: Instead of having to find information or entertainment, it will find you—and be exactly what you want or need at that moment…. In the Web era, you went on the Internet to find something—you sat down at a computer and tapped into search engines or shopping sites. In the new era, the network and the information will give you, unprompted, what you want depending on where you are and what you're doing."

The Internet2 Project

The first formal attempts to define the next-generation Internet came in 1996, with the formation of the Internet2 project. Administered by the University Corporation for Advanced Internet Development (UCAID), Internet2 is a consortium of more than 170 high-speed networks belonging to universities, corporations, and government agencies. These networks, which are linked together by fiber-optic backbones, are capable of transmitting data at speeds of 2.4 gigabits per second. That's about 45,000 times faster than information is transmitted on a typical 56K modem, or a telephone connection to the Internet.

Since coming online in 1999, the Internet2 project has provided a forum for advanced networking experiments. One of the participants' main goals involves creating new applications that cannot run on the existing Internet, and then developing the infrastructure necessary to support them. "What we need in higher education is a place to take bright ideas and see whether they're viable, to explore new modes of instruction, new ways of collaborating around the arts and performance," explained Ted Hanss, director of applications development for Internet2, in *Discover*. "Internet2 is structured to allow people to connect with one another without loss of nuance, whether it is the raised eyebrow or the fidelity of the musical piece you're playing."

The Internet2 project has led to important advances in several scientific fields of endeavor. For example, the network allows scientists to share access to sophisticated and expensive tools like electron microscopes and high-powered telescopes. It also enables doctors to manipulate high-resolution, three-dimensional images of body scans and even to simulate surgery.

The project also helped networking experts to design and test Internet Protocol version 6 (IPv6), an upgrade of the venerable TCP/IP protocol that governs communication between computers over the Internet. IPv6 offers improved speed and security as well as a vast increase in the number of IP addresses available. The latter development could come into play quickly, since a growing variety of consumer electronic devices requiring IP addresses have been connected to the Internet. Many experts have expressed concern that the number of currently available Internet addresses will soon prove insufficient to meet demand. Implementation of IPv6 requires a complex upgrade of routers and other equipment that forms the backbone of the Internet. This upgrade was ongoing in 2004. When complete, however, it promises to speed the process of integrating new technologies with the Internet.

Technologies Driving Future Changes

By 2004, a number of new technologies had emerged that appeared likely to drive future changes in the Internet. As of July, for example, half of all the American homes with Internet access—and an overwhelming majority of schools and businesses—used broadband connections, such as digital subscriber lines (DSL), cable, satellite, and wireless fidelity (Wi-Fi) systems. The spread of broadband, with its significantly faster download speeds, has encouraged content providers to design more sophisticated offerings. Experts

The Internet continues to evolve rapidly thanks to technological advances such as this microprocessor for cell phones that uses advances "wireless-Internet-on-a-chip" technology.

predict that bandwidth will continue to increase while also becoming less expensive, eventually allowing Internet users to receive high-resolution audio and video online.

Another important new technology is wireless networking, in which there is no physical connection between computers—instead, the computers communicate using radio-frequency signals. As wireless networking technology has improved, some analysts have claimed that people will soon enjoy the same mobility for Internet communications that they have with their cellular phones. Some predict that Wi-Max—a future generation of wireless fidelity—will eventually replace Wi-Fi, giving wireless connectivity the capacity to cover entire cities rather than small local areas.

Global positioning systems (GPS) have been used for military purposes for many years. GPS is a satellite-based navigation system that allows users to pinpoint a location within a few yards. Only in the last decade, however, has the U.S. military declassified its satellite network, allowing civilians access to the most accurate locators and measurements. That decision led to the development of small, affordable GPS receivers with detailed mapping features. These devices are commonly connected to the Internet, allowing users to download maps and directions from the Web. In the future, it is believed that this technology will increasingly be used by networks to track the position of users.

Radio-frequency identification (RFID) technology involves embedding tiny electronic transmitters on objects. These tags identify the object they are attached to, sending constant radio signals to the network regarding its status and location. As RFID becomes more prevalent, experts predict that significant portions of our environment will be tracked on the Internet. The combination of GPS and RFID will thus let the network know where a user is located, as well as the location of nearby objects. The next generation of RFID technology—already in the works—involves tiny silicon chips called "smart dust." These chips may be incorporated into such vital equipment as roads, bridges, and medical machinery. Once embedded, they will monitor the integrity of the structure or equipment. In cases where that integrity is compromised by malfunction or other damage, they will relay that information to technicians through wireless Internet connections.

The Internet's capacity to transform communications is being extended to spoken conversations as well through the development of Voice-over-Internet Protocol (VoIP), which breaks voice transmissions into packets of data that can be sent over the Internet. Since it came into use in 2002, VoIP has enabled users to save valuable bandwidth while also avoiding long-distance telephone charges. Some experts believe that the service will soon become available for PDAs and other Web-enabled devices, and may eventually replace traditional telephone service.

Avatar technology already enables Internet users to adopt an animated persona while participating in specially designed chat rooms. Users control their avatars' movements and expressions as they interact with other characters in a virtual social setting. In the future, improvements in three-dimensional graphics and tactile feedback systems are expected to lead to even more advanced virtual reality applications on the Internet. "Virtual reality applications will not only better and better reflect the natural world, they will also have the fluidity, flexibility, and speed of the digital world, layered on the Internet, and so will be used to create apparently magical environments of types we can only now begin to imagine," according to "The Living Internet," an authoritative online history of the Internet written by Bill Stewart. "These increasingly sophisticated virtual experiences will continue to change how we understand the nature of reality, experience, art, and human relations."

The Integration of Technologies

A number of Internet pioneers consider the integration of other machines with the Web to be the most likely future evolution of network technology. As

U.S. Internet Use from Any Location by Individuals Age 3 and Older			
	Internet Users (Percent)		Lives in a Broadband Household (Percent)
	Sept. 2001	Oct. 2003	Oct. 2003
TOTAL POPULATION	**55.1**	**58.7**	**22.8**
Gender			
Male	55.2	58.2	23.9
Female	55.0	59.2	21.8
Race/Ethnicity[a]			
White[b]	61.3	65.1	25.7
White Alone	n/a	65.1	25.7
Black[c]	41.1	45.6	14.2
Black Alone	n/a	45.2	13.9
Asian Amer. & Pac. Isl.[d]	62.5	63.1	34.2
Asian Amer. & Pac. Isl. Alone	n/a	63.0	34.7
Hispanic (of any race)	33.4	37.2	12.6
Employment Status			
Employed[e]	66.6	70.7	26.0
Not Employed (unemployed or NLF)[e]	38.0	42.8	16.1
Family Income			
Less than $15,000	25.9	31.2	7.5
$15,000-$24,999	34.4	38.0	9.3
$25,000-$34,999	45.3	48.9	13.4
$35,000-$49,999	58.3	62.1	19.0
$50,000-$74,999	68.9	71.8	27.9
$75,000 & above	80.4	82.9	45.4
$75,000-$99,999[f]	n/a	79.8	36.8
$100,000-$149,999[f]	n/a	85.1	49.3
$150,000 & above[f]	n/a	86.1	57.7
Educational Attainment[g]			
Less Than High School	13.7	15.5	5.9
High School Diploma / GED	41.1	44.5	14.5
Some College	63.5	68.6	23.7
Bachelor's Degree	82.2	84.9	34.9
Beyond Bachelor's Degree	85.0	88.0	38.0
Age Group			
Age 3-4	17.6	19.9	22.0
Age 5-9	41.0	42.0	24.1
Age10-13	66.7	67.3	25.8
Age14-17	76.4	78.8	28.3
Age 18-24	66.6	70.6	25.5

U.S. Internet Use from Any Location by Individuals Age 3 and Older			
	Internet Users (Percent)		Lives in a Broadband Household (Percent)
	Sept. 2001	Oct. 2003	Oct. 2003
Age Group (cont.)			
In School	85.4	86.7	33.8
Not in School	54.0	58.2	19.0
Age 25-49	65.0	68.0	25.9
In Labor Force	68.4	71.7	26.8
Not in Labor Force	47.1	49.7	21.1
Age 50+	38.3	44.8	15.9
In Labor Force	58.0	64.4	22.6
Not in Labor Force	22.2	27.6	10.1
Location of the Person's Household			
Rural	54.1	57.2	
Urban	55.5	59.2	
Urban Not Central City	58.8	62.5	
Urban Central City	50.3	54.0	
Household Type in Which the Individual Lives[h]			
Married Couple w/Children < 18 Years Old	63.5	65.3	29.3
Male Householder w/Children < 18 Years Old	46.8	50.3	19.4
Female Householder w/Children < 18 Years Old	46.6	51.4	14.8
Households without Children	51.8	56.7	20.7
Non-Family Household	48.3	53.1	17.3
Location of Internet Use			
Only At Home	19.0	19.0	
Only Outside the Home	11.8	11.6	

n/a = Not Available

a In 2003 respondents were able to choose multiple racial categories. Thus, 2003 race data are not strictly comparable with data from previous surveys.

b For 2003, "White" should be read as "White alone or in combination with other racial categories, non-Hispanic."

c For 2003, "Black" should be read as "Black alone or in combination with other racial categories, non-Hispanic."

d For 2003, "Asian Amer. & Pac. Isl." should be read as "Asian American and Pacific Islanders alone or in combination with other racial categories, non-Hispanic."

e Age 16 and Older. NLF=Not in the labor force.

f The October 2003 Current Population Survey had income categories above $75,000 that were not previously available.

g Age 25 and older.

h The male and female categories refer to family households where a spouse is not present.

Source: U.S. Department of Commerce's *A Nation Online: Entering the Broadband Age.*

Tim Berners-Lee, inventor of the World Wide Web, told *USA Today:* "The Web can reach its full potential only if it becomes a place where data can be shared and processed by automated tools as well as by people." Many experts believe that a wide variety of everyday electronic devices—including cars, telephones, cameras, TVs, household appliances, consumer electronics, and home security systems—will eventually be connected to the Internet, creating an integrated system of data communications that users can access and control from anywhere.

"The Internet is still synonymous with people talking to other people, but we're seeing a fundamental shift," Paul Saffo, director of the Institute of the Future, explained in *FutureNet.* "The biggest growth in the Internet is not in people-to-people, but in machine-to-machine. So what we're going to see in the next 10 years is that human-to-human communication is going to become an increasingly smaller proportion of the total Internet traffic.... [The first decade of the 21st century] is being shaped by the advent of cheap sensors. We're basically in the process of hanging eyes and ears and sensory organs on our computers and networks and asking them to observe the world on our behalf, and manipulate that information on our behalf."

Many experts also believe that "follow-me" Internet access services will become widely available, allowing users to maintain a constant Internet connection through a variety of devices—including telephones, personal digital assistants (PDAs), and televisions—depending on where they are. According to Larry Roberts, who directed the ARPANET project in the 1960s, "People will have one channel in their house and they won't have cable, or satellite, or Internet separately. It will be a single line—a single line that handles everything," he predicted in *FutureNet.*

The integration of machines and technologies with the Internet promises to impact users' lives in myriad ways. The following examples provide a glimpse of what the future might hold:

- You may be able to surf the Web in the shower using a waterproof touchpad screen, enabling you to get a weather forecast, check your e-mail, and set up your home security system before you leave the house.

- You may wear plasma clothing that will give you the capacity to change your wardrobe instantly, simply by wirelessly downloading new outfits from the Internet.

- Optical recognition software may help you remember the names and positions of everyone attending a meeting or a party.

- As you drive home, your house may sense your impending arrival and prepare itself according to your preferences: resetting the thermostat, preheating the oven, turning on the television, and opening the garage door.

- Sensors within your car may take steps to mitigate a problem before you even become aware of it: sending details to a nearby repair shop, arranging for a tow truck, and renting a replacement vehicle.

- You may be able to use a handheld wireless device to take an inventory of all the items in your refrigerator or pantry and create a list of recipes that can be made using those items.

- If you are running low on food, your refrigerator may automatically e-mail a shopping list to your local supermarket and check your schedule for a convenient delivery time.

- The picture frames in your home may be linked to an online gallery of digital photos of your family and friends, allowing you to rotate the displays constantly or change them whenever you wish.

- All of the electronic devices and appliances in your home may be controlled through a WiFi remote control that automatically downloads any necessary security patches and upgrades for you.

While such possibilities hold appeal for some people, others question their usefulness. One such skeptic is Bob Kahn, the computer scientist who gave the first public demonstration of the ARPANET and helped develop the TCP/IP protocol. As Kahn noted in *FutureNet,* "I'm not sure what you would do with your refrigerator over the Internet, other than use it as a display, and I'm skeptical that that is going to happen any time soon. Will it communicate with services to reorder? Well, maybe the milk is all there, but it went sour, or what happens when someone replaces the milk where it doesn't belong?"

Still other experts predict that the Internet will become increasingly integrated not only with other machines, but with human beings as well. That view was expressed by Leonard Kleinrock, who wrote the first academic paper describing packet-switching theory and oversaw installation of the first node of

A "Father of the Internet"
Explains the Rapid Pace of Change

Vinton Cerf, who helped design vital Internet protocols in the 1960s and 1970s, has watched the Internet evolve for more than 30 years. In an interview with Sally Richards for *FutureNet: The Past, Present, and Future of the Internet as Told by Its Creators and Visionaries,* Cerf gave his perspective on why the network has developed and changed so rapidly.

There are millions of people out there, just like millions of ants on an anthill; if you ever watch an anthill—millions of ants go running around and mostly on any given day most of them don't find anything interesting, but there are so darn many ants that every day a few of them find something interesting and they bring it back to the anthill. The Internet is very much like that. There are hundreds of millions of people out there using it and many of them are trying experiments out; they are ISPs, or researchers, and most of them don't have very interesting results. But because there are so many on the Net, every day 3, or 4, or 10 things happen that are significant— important breakthroughs, new applications coming up. As a result, it feels like we are rushing headlong into the future.... It's literally the cumulative effect of everybody trying things out and some of them finding something that makes the Net seem like it's changing so rapidly.

the ARPANET at UCLA. Kleinrock told *FutureNet* that the Internet of the future "will be invisible. It will literally become part of the environment and users won't even think of it. I think it will be part of our biology—embedded." He believes that future technological advances will allow Web-enabled medical devices to be implanted in the human body. He foresees such devices being used to monitor chronic conditions, dispense drugs, and provide doctors with information about a person's medical history and current health status.

Some people take the idea of biological-technological integration even further, claiming that individuals might someday be connected together through the Internet. "I think 10 or 20 years from now it won't be anything like what we have today," futurist Bob Glass stated in *FutureNet*. "I think we'll have some kind of technology aura with our personal information that will somehow be hooked up to every other aura. I think the Internet becomes the backbone of what will become nanotechnology. With this technology, if I'm out there on the street my aura will read yours and yours will read mine, and it'll give us some information about each other."

Potential Problems and Obstacles

Although the possible future applications of Internet technology offer many benefits, they also come with potential drawbacks—both on an individual level and on a global scale. "This technology is going to become more pervasive in our lives," Bran Ferren noted in *Discover*. "It will appear on things we wear, on things we see, in cars we drive. And it brings with it both good and bad. You cannot go a week without reading about some new virus that is taking down systems, wiping out hard drives, and costing us millions of dollars." As Saffo explained in *FutureNet*, "Everything new always comes with a hidden curse and new technologies are always a mixed bag—they solve old problems, they create new opportunities, and then, in the process, they create new problems we didn't anticipate. The Internet is no different than any other technology in this regard. The only difference is that … with the Internet there's a lot more suspense and uncertainty." Indeed, observers foresee potential pitfalls associated with continued integration of Internet technology into all corners of daily existence. These pitfalls include loss of privacy, increased social isolation and parallel erosion of relationships in physical communities, and increased work and social obligations associated with always being "on the grid."

On a global level, the Internet has the potential to fundamentally change the future of human relations. "A better-informed humanity will make better macro-level decisions, and an increasingly integrated world will drive international relations toward a global focus," predicted "The Living Internet." "Attachments to countries will marginally decrease, and attachments to the Earth as a shared resource will significantly increase."

Yet as the Internet continues to break down geographic boundaries, some experts worry about its effect on international relations, government authority, and individual rights and freedoms. "In a networked world, what will be the nature of government power? The fact that the Internet spans the world, and is indifferent to borders, squarely challenges the idea of geographically specific legal jurisdictions that has been the basis of the nation state," stated the *Economist*. "As the growing power of electronic technology makes it possible to conduct more social interactions on a global network, the Internet will force governments to decide whether they should act alone or together on a wide array of issues, from law enforcement to tax collection to the regulation of obscenity."

In any case, there is no doubt that the Internet revolution will continue to have profound effects on human society in the future. "We all live in the Internet society now, whether or not we spend any time online," the *Economist* concluded. "The future will bring exciting, disorienting change as electronic communication reaches ever deeper into everyone's life. The prizes will be great. A more productive and safer society is possible. But things could also go nastily wrong."

BIOGRAPHIES

Marc Andreessen (1971-)

Computer Programmer Who Created Early Browsers, Including Mosaic and Netscape Navigator

Marc Andreessen was born in July 1971 in the small town of New Lisbon, Wisconsin. His father, Lowell, was an agriculturalist, while his mother, Patricia, worked for a mail-order catalog retailer. Andreessen showed an affinity for computers and technology from an early age. In grade school he devoured numerous books on computer-related subjects, and he even put together a program on the school's computer to assist him with his math homework. Unfortunately, the program was not saved on a disk, so it was lost when the school custodian shut the building's power off at the end of the day.

A top student in high school, Andreessen enrolled at the University of Illinois after earning his diploma. He initially planned to major in electrical engineering, but his fascination with computers eventually led him to concentrate on computer science, earning a bachelor of science degree in the subject in 1993.

Creating the Mosaic Browser

The origins of Andreessen's revolutionary software to facilitate browsing the World Wide Web can be traced back to the National Center for Supercomputing Applications (NCSA). Andreessen worked at this research center on the Illinois campus to make pocket money as an intern. It was at NCSA that he met programmer Eric Bina. Together, the men devised a graphical interface for navigating the World Wide Web, which then required users to type in complicated series of text-based commands. At the time, the Web was little-known outside the halls of academia and research institutions. "What we were trying to do was just put a human face on the Internet," Andreessen later recalled in *Nerds 2.0.1*.

Andreessen and Bina succeeded spectacularly in achieving this goal. The program they devised, called Mosaic, ushered in a new era of text, graphics, and sound on the Internet. Posted for free on the Internet in March 1993, Mosaic offered "the possibility of a world of pictures and colors," wrote John Motavalli in *Bamboozled at the Revolution.* "It was akin to the moment radio became TV, and almost as dramatic."

Mosaic altered the online world at breakneck speed. "Once it [gathered momentum,]" reported Robert Reid in *Architects of the Web,* "it was almost unstoppable. Because as more and more people started using the Web, the information that was posted there was able to reach bigger and bigger audiences. This of course attracted more information providers, who piled the Web's shelf higher and higher with more information and content, which in turn attracted even more people, which in turn attracted even more information."

Andreessen quickly recognized that the growing popularity of Mosaic and the wider Web also had potentially profound financial implications. "The number of Mosaic users went from originally twelve to a hundred to a thousand to ten thousand to somewhere in the order of a million by the end of 1993," he observed in *Nerds 2.0.1.* "So it didn't take a whole lot of imagination to figure out that if it kept doubling for the next couple of years that it was going to be a five-, ten-million person environment, which starts to be an interesting commercial opportunity."

Launching Netscape

In 1994 Andreessen hooked up with Jim Clark, founder of Silicon Graphics, to develop Mosaic into a commercial entity. Their endeavor coalesced into a company called Netscape Communications after the NCSA voiced objections to their appropriation of the Mosaic name. Netscape attracted other talented people as well, including Bina, Chris Houck, Rob McCool, Jon Mittelhauser, Lou Montulli, and Aleks Totic.

In October 1994 Andreessen, Clark, and the Netscape staff released a new and vastly superior form of the Mosaic browser, now called Netscape Navigator, on the Internet for no charge. Bristling with new security measures, improved graphics, and far greater speed than Andreessen's original program, it was compatible with Unix, Windows, and Macintosh operating systems, and it took Internet-accessibility to a new and exciting level. As Navigator was snapped up by the proliferating ranks of Internet "surfers," Andreessen oversaw the development of other profitable Netscape goods and services, all the while maintaining a work environment that was both collegial and dynamic.

In 1995 Netscape held a historic initial public stock offering (IPO) that made Andreessen an instant multi-millionaire. The heady success of the IPO also heralded a new era in American investment. As Reid wrote in *Architects of the Web,* "Netscape's dramatic IPO put the Internet indelibly on the map with millions of people who hadn't yet been there…. The Net was now a front-page land that raced infant companies to the public market; one where people *got rich!* in months flat. To some this made it a realm of inspiring promise; to many others, one of unconscionable hype. But whatever it was, the Internet would never again be a *huh?* to the business mainstream."

Dueling with Microsoft

But soon the computer software giant Microsoft Corporation became interested in the Web browser market. In 1996 Microsoft signaled its intention to enter the lucrative Web browser sweepstakes and challenge Netscape's position of market supremacy. Andreessen and Netscape braced for the onslaught, even as they opened new offices, expanded their product line, and shored up their programming muscle. In September 1997 Microsoft launched its Internet Explorer 4.0 browser. Significantly, Microsoft distributed the browser by "bundling" it with Windows. In other words, it gave away its browser software with copies of its operating system, which runs on over 90 percent of PCs on the market. In so doing, Microsoft was potentially taking a sizable share of Netscape's market. This strategy was devastatingly successful, eroding Netscape Navigator's market share within a matter of weeks.

Andreessen and his staff scrambled to blunt Microsoft's charge through a variety of innovative measures. But in the end Microsoft usurped Netscape's place as the best-selling Web browser. The U.S. Justice Department and several states eventually filed suit against Microsoft on behalf of Netscape and other competitors, charging the software giant with using its monopoly on operating systems to unfairly corner the browser market. (In June 2000 Microsoft was found to be in violation of U.S. antitrust laws, and in November 2001 the company reached a settlement with the Justice Department that did not materially alter Explorer's status as the world's leading Web browser.)

But while this legal battle was winding its way through the courts, Netscape's business fortunes continued to decline. In 1999 America Online (AOL), the largest online service provider in the United States, acquired Netscape for about $4.2 billion.

105

Andreessen briefly served as AOL's chief technology executive, but by year's end he had resigned and launched a new company. This firm, Loud-Cloud, initially provided long-term consulting and technology development services to large companies with a significant financial stake on the Internet. But Andreessen later changed the company name to Opsware, and its emphasis is now on selling products that enable firms to manage multiple computer networks from anywhere.

Andreessen remains optimistic about the future of information technology. "Right now, today, with a little luck and brains and timing, any kid with a computer can do what Netscape has done," he said. "There are no barriers to entry anymore. Any kid can spark a revolution." He also believes that the Internet is poised to experience new growth and innovation in the coming years. "Any new technology tends to go through a 25-year adoption cycle," he told *Wired.com*. "I look at what happened from 1975 to 1985, the first 10 years of the PC adoption cycle. There was huge over-investment in the early 1980s. In the late '80s there was a huge crash, and the real build-out was from 1990 to 2000. With the Internet, we're really 10 years into what will ultimately look like a 25-year cycle from invention to full implementation."

Sources

Glasner, Joanna. "Conversation with Marc Andreessen." *Wired.com,* February 14, 2003. Available online at http://www.wired.com/news/business/0,1367,57661,00.html.

Randall, Neil. *The Soul of the Internet: Net Gods, Netizens, and the Wiring of the World.* New York: International Thompson Computer Press, 1997.

Reid, Robert H. *Architects of the Web: 1,000 Days that Built the Future of Business.* New York: Wiley, 1997.

Segaller, Stephen. *Nerds 2.0.1: A Brief History of the Internet.* New York: TV Books, 1998.

Tetzeli, Rick. "What It's Really Like to Be Marc Andreessen." *Fortune,* December 9, 1996.

Tim Berners-Lee (1955-)
Creator of the World Wide Web

Tim Berners-Lee was born on June 8, 1955, in London, England. His parents, Conway and Mary Berners-Lee, were mathematicians who met in the early 1950s while working on the Ferranti Mark 1, England's first commercial computer.

Berners-Lee was fascinated by computers throughout his childhood and adolescence. As a student at Queen's College at Oxford University, he used a soldering iron, an old television set, and an assortment of electrical equipment to construct a primitive—but operational—computer. After graduating in 1976 with a bachelor's degree in physics, he worked for several British firms as a software designer and telecommunications research engineer.

Creating Enquire

In 1980 Berners-Lee spent six months as a software consultant at CERN (Conseil Européen pour la Recherche Nucléaire), the European Laboratory for Particle Physics in Geneva, Switzerland. During his stay at CERN, he cobbled together a computer program for his own personal use that linked together the information in his daily schedule planner, his address book, and papers and documents on which he was working. He called this experimental program "Enquire," after *Enquire Within Upon Everything,* a Victorian-era encyclopedia of sorts that he recalled from his childhood.

The Enquire program actually utilized a programming innovation devised nearly two decades earlier by a Harvard University programmer named Ted Nelson. Under this concept, dubbed "hypertext" by Nelson, any word or phrase in one electronic document could be outfitted with embedded codes that would enable it to link to another part of the document—or to an entirely different document, for that matter.

Building on this conceptual foundation, Berners-Lee established a series of electronic links, first between the various documents in his own computer, and then to the computers of the hundreds of other scientists working at the vast CERN nuclear research facilities. These links created a veritable "web" of information through which Berners-Lee could move quite freely (at this point in time, the computer mouse had not yet been invented, so instead of the "point and click" system used by modern computer users, he had to manually key in the link identifiers). This program, quietly cobbled together over a period of a few months, would eventually become the conceptual foundation for the future development of the World Wide Web.

In 1981 Berners-Lee moved on to Image Computer Systems in England. He spent the next three years there, designing hardware and communications software for printers, but in 1984 he received an invitation to join the staff at CERN. He quickly accepted the offer and returned to Geneva, where he began working on developing new information systems for the institution.

Around the time that Berners-Lee returned to CERN, the research facility connected its computers to a growing worldwide network that became known as the Internet. Over the next several years, Berners-Lee became increasingly focused on finding ways to access information stored on remote computers that were also connected to the Internet. Returning to his Enquire program as a starting point, he began fleshing out the vital communication protocols needed for navigating the Internet and transmitting documents across the network. "I happened to come along … after hypertext and the Internet had come of age," he explained in *Weaving the Web*. "The task left to me was to marry them together." This work was never officially sanctioned by his supervisors at CERN, but they gave him quiet encouragement to pursue his ideas.

Weaving the World Wide Web

The fall of 1990 proved to be a particularly pivotal period in the development of the World Wide Web. It was during these autumn months that Berners-Lee invented Hypertext Markup Language (HTML), a coding system that identified various elements in a document, such as words, pictures, and sound. These codes became the language that allowed for the formatting of Web pages to include text, headings, graphics, and hypertext links. At the same time, Berners-Lee established a communication standard called Hypertext Transfer Protocol (HTTP), which allowed documents to be linked together across the Internet and retrieved in readable form from remote locations by special software programs (later known as Web browsers). Finally, he invented the Uniform Resource Locator (URL) system, which gave each document a unique "address" on the Internet.

As he neared completion of his work, Berners-Lee recognized on some level that his combination of software programs and networking protocols had the potential to create an electronic "web" of information capable of spanning the globe. Thus, after considering and discarding several possible names for his creation, he decided to call it the World Wide Web.

In the summer of 1991 Berners-Lee unveiled the World Wide Web to the public. Rather than trying to make money from his invention, however, he posted the software on the Internet for anyone to download free of charge. Several months later he formally relinquished all rights to the HTML, HTTP, and URL programs he had created, even though he and many others sensed that the Internet was on the cusp of explosive growth. Berners-Lee has never expressed any remorse about this decision in subsequent years, however. In fact, he strongly defends his idealistic choice. "What is maddening is the terrible notion that a person's value depends on how important and financially successful they are, and that is measured in terms of money," he wrote in *Weaving the Web*. "That suggests disrespect for the researchers across the globe developing ideas for the next leaps in science and technology. If your requirement is to make a large amount of money, then your options in life are rather small."

From 1991 to 1993 Berners-Lee further refined the design of the World Wide Web, absorbing feedback from users across the Internet. Meanwhile, adherents to his system were literally remaking the Internet with each passing day, using his programs to build exciting new Web sites and browsers to access them. Berners-Lee watched the whole thing unfold with understandable pride. "I think the main intention was to make the thing fly," he commented in Stephen Segaller's *Nerds 2.0.1*. "When you're really attached to a dream of how things could be, then you puruse that dream and it's very, very satisfying to see it work. The fact that the World Wide Web did work, I find is just exciting for itself. Exciting that you can have an idea and it can take off and it can happen. It means that dreamers all over the world should take off and not stop."

Director of the World Wide Web Consortium

In 1994 Berners-Lee accepted a position as a research scientist at the Laboratory for Computer Science (LCS) at the Massachusetts Institute of Technology (MIT). Shortly after arriving at MIT, he founded the World Wide

Web Consortium (W3C). Today, this consortium includes more than 300 companies that meet regularly to discuss Internet issues, coordinate Web development, and ensure that the Web's wealth of information continues to remain accessible to everyone. Berners-Lee continues to serve as the director of the W3C from his modest MIT offices.

In recognition of his enormous contributions to Internet technology, Berners-Lee has received numerous prestigious awards over the years. In 1999 *Time* magazine named him one of the "100 Most Influential Minds of the 20th Century," explaining that "unlike so many of the inventions that have moved the world, this one truly was the work of one man.... The World Wide Web is Berners-Lee's alone. He designed it. He loosed it on the world. And he more than anyone else has fought to keep it open, nonproprietary, and free." In December 2003 he was knighted by Britain's Queen Elizabeth II for his "services to the global development of the Internet," and in June 2004 Berners-Lee became the first-ever recipient of the Millennium Technology Prize, a $1.2 million cash prize presented by the Finnish Technology Award Foundation.

Berners-Lee has long been known as a semi-reclusive figure who avoids the trappings of fame. But while he is vigilant about protecting the privacy of himself and his family, he readily volunteers his thoughts on the future of the Internet and information technology. He expresses great optimism about the promise of new technological innovations, and speculates that today's Web will eventually evolve into what he calls the Semantic Web—a network in which data will have meaning to the computer, enabling it to make logical inferences and carry out routine research and analyses that currently blunt human creativity. "It's important that the Web help people be intuitive as well as analytical," he wrote in *Weaving the Web*. "If we succeed, creativity will arise across larger and more diverse groups."

Berners-Lee does, however, express concern about the potential erosion of the Web's longstanding universal access philosophy. He is troubled, for example, by growing speculation about the introduction of Web pages accessible only to people using certain browsers. "For me the fundamental Web is the Web of people," he declared in a 1999 address during the LCS's 35th anniversary celebration. "It's not the Web of machines talking to each other; it's not the network of machines talking to each other. It's not the Web of documents. Remember when machines talk to each other over some protocol, two machines are talking on behalf of two people. The Consortium has a whole technical domain 'Technology and Society' which recognizes that, at the end of the day, if we're not doing something for the Web of people, then we're really not doing something useful at all."

Sources

Berners-Lee, Tim, with Mark Fischetti. *Weaving the Web: The Original Design and Ultimate Destiny of the World Wide Web by Its Inventor.* New York: HarperCollins, 1999.

Berners-Lee, Tim. Transcript of speech delivered at MIT Laboratory for Computer Science 35th Anniversary celebrations, April 1999. Available online at http://www.w3.org/1999/04/13-tbl.html.

Henderson, Harry. *History Makers: Pioneers of the Internet.* San Diego: Lucent, 2002.

Segaller, Stephen. *Nerds 2.0.1: A Brief History of the Internet.* New York: TV Books, 1998.

Sergey Brin (1973-)
Larry Page (1973-)
Co-Founders of Google Internet Search Engine

Sergey Brin and Larry Page—co-founders of Google, which became the biggest and most influential search engine in the opening years of the twenty-first century—arrived at their positions from very different circumstances. Brin was born on August 21, 1973, in Moscow in the former Soviet Union. His family moved to the United States when he was six years old. Page, meanwhile, was born in 1973 in East Lansing, Michigan. Both of his parents were heavily involved in computer science—his mother as a database consultant and his father as a professor of computer science at Michigan State University.

Brin earned bachelor's degrees in math and computer science from the University of Maryland, while Page received his undergraduate education at the University of Michigan. They first met in the computer science doctoral program at Stanford University. In 1996 the two men collaborated on an academic research project on Internet searching that they dubbed "BackRub"—named for its emphasis on analyzing the "back links" pointing to a given Web site. In essence, their project sought to find ways of prioritizing search results so that rankings were based on Web site popularity and relevance rather than repetition of search terms within a given Web site.

At the time, most search engines were compiled by "spiders," automated devices that crawled across the Web and created a database of terms appearing on Web sites. When users searched for a specific term, the search engines returned a list of sites in which the term appeared. The approach taken by Brin and Page expanded upon this idea to index not only terms, but also the popularity and relevance of a given Web site, based on the number of links it received from other sites. This allowed BackRub to return more accurate and useful search results.

The results of the project were so startling that Page and Brin decided that their system had viable commercial possibilities. With that in mind, they left Stanford's Ph.D. program to explore a new business venture. The duo established Page's dormitory room as their data center, rented out a business office, and began calling on potential buyers of their new search technology.

Unable to attract buyers, Brin and Page ultimately decided to launch their own search engine company. Naming their company Google Inc., they formally opened for business on September 7, 1998, at modest facilities in Menlo Park, California. Within a matter of weeks, business and Internet media were hailing the Google search engine as a revolutionary advance in Web development and navigation. In late 1999, for example, *PC Magazine* declared that "Google is an almost frighteningly accurate search engine. Our testing found that the quality of the results matches or exceeds that of every other site tested."

In February 1999 the company relocated to Palo Alto, California. Over the next several months it announced the signing of several commercial search customers and an infusion of $25 million from Silicon Valley's two leading venture capital firms, Sequoia Capital and Kleiner Parkers. The company continued to expand, relocating to its current headquarters in Mountain View, California, and consolidating its gains in cyberspace. In June 2000 the company founded by Brin and Page a mere two years earlier officially became the world's largest search engine with its introduction of a billion-page index. The company's financial fortunes were given a further boost by the introduction of a keyword-targeted advertising program.

By the end of 2000, Google was handling more than 100 million search queries daily. In the aftermath of the 2000 dot.com collapse, it stood far above virtually all other major Internet businesses in terms of financial health. Over the next two years it became even more firmly entrenched as an Internet giant, establishing partnerships around the world with companies including Yahoo!, NEC, and America Online. The company's leadership also was augmented during this time by the arrival of Eric E. Schmidt, who became chairman and chief executive officer. Brin served as president of technology, while Page served as president of product.

By 2003 it was estimated that three-quarters of all Internet searches were being done via Google. Its popularity was reflected in its financial performance, as it turned more than $100 million in profit on revenues of just under $1 billion. The company's continued upward trajectory, both in terms of size and performance, fed rampant speculation that the company might soon make the transition to a publicly held company.

In 2004 Google announced plans for an initial public offering (IPO) of stock that attracted interest from investors all over the world. Some analysts complained about the nature of the IPO, noting that Brin and Page had devised a multi-tiered value system for shares. Their system ensured that they would continue to control the strategic direction of the company and thus could preserve the idealistic, creative company culture they had cultivated over the years. But many others described the Google IPO as an enticing one. "Let's face it—it's good to be Google," observed *Newsweek:*

> Every minute, worldwide, in 90 languages, the index of this Internet-based search engine created by these Stanford doctoral dropouts is probed more than 138,000 times. In the course of a day, that's over 200 million searches of 7 billion Web pages, images, and discussion-group postings…. Amazingly, the majority of these queries evoke satisfactory, even revelatory, results. Google has changed the way the world finds things out, and enticed it to look for things previously considered unfindable.

On August 19 the Google IPO took place, with investors able to claim a piece of the company at $85 a share. The offering made instant billionaires of both Page and Brin, and in the weeks immediately following the IPO the stock price of Google surged upward on the strength of very strong financial results.

Given the historic volatility of Internet stocks and business fortunes, some analysts wonder whether Google's current health and vitality can be sustained over the long term. But others note that in Schmidt, Brin, and Page, the company has stable and proven leadership. In addition, Web watchers note the company's continuous technological improvements, such as the capacity to search for books, news, and products as well as Web sites, and a downloadable desktop search tool that allows users to search hard drives. Such features are likely to keep Google at the top of the cyberspace hierarchy for some time to come.

Sources

Cummings, Betsy. "Beating the Odds." *Sales & Marketing Management,* March 2002.
"Google Corporate Information, Google History." *Google.com,* undated. Available online at www.google.com/corporate/history.html.
Levy, Steven, Brad Stone, and Peter Suciu. "All Eyes on Google." *Newsweek,* March 29, 2004.
Marshall, Matt. "Google Founders' Brashness Sparks Debate." *San Jose Mercury News,* August 18, 2004.
"Top Ten Technology Innovators: Larry Page and Sergey Brin." *InfoWorld,* March 4, 2002.

Steve Case (1958-)
Co-Founder of America Online (AOL)

Stephen McConnell Case was born in Honolulu, Hawaii, on August 21, 1958. He was the third of four children born to Daniel Case Jr., a corporate attorney, and Carol Case, an elementary school teacher and stay-at-home mom. As a youth Case was by all accounts an indifferent student, but an energetic entrepreneur. During his high school and college years he launched a wide variety of businesses and explored various student body leadership positions. He failed in some of these endeavors—occasionally in spectacular fashion—but these setbacks did not dampen his enthusiasm for the world of business.

Case attended Williams College in Williamstown, Massachusetts, graduating in 1980 with a bachelor's degree in political science. He promptly joined Procter & Gamble as an assistant brand manager, then moved on to Wichita, Kansas, where he took a management position with Pizza Hut. In 1982 he made a fateful purchase that has since been recounted time and again in America Online (AOL) lore. He bought a bulky Kaypro II personal computer and a modem, then laid out $100 for a subscription to the Source, the first online service for consumers. "When I finally logged in and found myself linked to people all over the country from this sorry little apartment in Wichita, it was just exhilarating," Case recalled. This epiphany would have a seismic impact not only on Case's future career, but on the development of the Internet.

The Birth of AOL

In 1983 Case joined Control Video Corporation, a small company that was focused on providing online gaming services to Atari computer owners. Over the next few years, the company struggled to survive, enduring wrenching financial losses and a flurry of management shakeups. When the dust finally cleared in 1985, the company had a new name (Quantum Computer Services) and new leadership (Jim Kimsey as CEO and Case as director of marketing). It also had a new business emphasis, offering "Q-Link" online services for owners of Commodore 64 computers. This was the modest beginning of what would become the America Online empire.

Over the next several years, Case registered a series of stunning business successes that transformed Quantum from a minor industry player into a fast-rising phenomenon. These successes—businesses deals in which the company secured deals to build proprietary online services for industry giants like Apple Computer, Tandy, and IBM—were almost entirely due to Case's marketing acumen and salesmanship.

In 1991 the company formally changed its name to America Online. Kimsey became chairman, paving the way for Case to take the title of CEO. Several months later, though, as the company prepared to unveil an initial public offering (IPO) of shares on the stock market, Case returned the CEO title to Kimsey. This maneuver was meant to reassure potential investors who might have been put off by Case's relative youth, and it proved to be a temporary measure. In March 1992, with the IPO behind them, Case reclaimed his CEO title.

During this period, AOL ranked far behind the online services CompuServe and Prodigy in terms of market share. But Case spearheaded an ingenious marketing campaign that closed the gap quickly. The centerpiece of Case's strategy was mass mailings of disks of AOL software to neighborhoods across America. These mailings, which offered free trial service, proved enormously effective in attracting new customers. AOL consolidated these gains in subsequent months by adding new chat room, bulletin board, e-mail, and search service options.

Perhaps more importantly, Case successfully cloaked the sometimes intimidating aura of the Internet in a friendly, easily understood package. At that time, the Internet was not widely used by people who were not computer savvy. Many people found it confusing and difficult to figure out how to get connected. "[Case] buried the old competition by promoting AOL as a simple on-line service for the masses, by demystifying it and making it so innocuous that no one was intimidated by the underlying bauds and megabytes," wrote Nina Munk in *Vanity Fair.*

In the early years, numerous industry analysts predicted that Case and AOL were living on borrowed time, doomed to be swallowed up or swept aside by Microsoft or one of the other industry giants. None of these predictions came to pass, though the company did receive a significant scare in the mid-1990s when several competing Internet service providers began to lure AOL customers away by offering plans with unlimited access for a flat rate. Case responded by instituting an inexpensive flat rate program that was enormously popular. The response, in fact, was so great that the AOL system was temporarily overwhelmed. But the company feverishly made the necessary adjustments and sailed on, with Case's reputation further enhanced. Afterward, in fact, business writer Kara Swisher described Case as "the Rasputin of the Internet, with no one able to deliver the long-expected deathblow."

In 1998 AOL acquired CompuServe, and one year later it swallowed up Netscape Communications. By 1999 America Online was a business behemoth, registering $6.9 billion in revenue (up from $30 million only seven years earlier) and 15,000 employees (up from 250 in 1992). Like numerous other Internet and high-tech companies during this period, it also saw its stock value soar as investors rushed to get in on the "dot.com" boom. On December 13, 1999, AOL stock hit an all-time high of $94, making the company worth more than General Motors and Ford Motor Company combined. Its leader, meanwhile, was being touted as one of the business emperors of the dawning Internet age.

A Fateful Merger

In January 2000 Case announced that AOL intended to buy Time Warner, a global media empire, for as much as $164 billion in stock (the exact value would be determined by the stock prices of the two entities). According to Case, the rationale of the purchase was quite simple: AOL wanted to become more diversified in the event of a downturn in the value of Internet-related stocks, and it wanted to add to its arsenal of weapons when doing battle against Microsoft and other major industry players. He and others believed that by acquiring Time Warner's immensely valuable media content holdings, AOL could establish profitable new revenue streams on the Internet.

Two months later, AOL's acquisition of Time Warner created the world's most powerful media-and-entertainment corporate entity. Then the "dot.com" bubble burst and Internet stocks plummeted in value. Within a matter of days, it was clear that AOL had acted in the nick of time; if it had waited even three months longer to buy Time Warner, it would not have had nearly the financial resources needed. This knowledge delighted AOL shareholders but elicited far different reactions from Time Warner shareholders and employees, who were stunned by dramatic drops in the value of their stocks and retirement accounts.

The controversy, coupled with difficulties in merging the divergent corporate cultures of AOL and Time Warner, eventually led to the forced departures of Time Warner CEO Gerald Levin, COO Robert Pittman, and various other top executives. Case remained chairman of AOL Time Warner, but he was nearly invisible for much of this time, partly because of his distant management style and partly because he spent a lot of time with his brother, who was dying. As a result, Case eventually became what business writer Nina Munk called "the last man standing—a target for the accumulated ill will of employees and investors unappeased by the previous bloodlettings."

Some people tried to paint Case as a slick shyster who pulled a fast one with the AOL Time Warner merger. But other observers had a different view. *Business Week,* for example, declared that "Case was a Net pioneer who made it possible for millions of Americans to gain access to a new technology for $20 a month. That he persuaded gullible folks at Time Warner to accept AOL's dreamy stock valuation in 2000 and part with their magazine, movie, and cable assets cheaply, makes him a smart businessman, not a villain."

Leaves AOL Time Warner

After three unhappy years as chairman of AOL Time Warner Inc., Case resigned from the company in January 2003. At the time of his resignation, AOL had 35 million worldwide subscribers, nearly four times the number of subscribers at runner-up MSN. But it had suffered a 70 percent loss in value since the merger, and analysts contended that it had fallen behind competitors in such critical areas as broadband technology, e-mail, instant messaging, and other services.

Despite the circumstances under which Case left, speculation continues to percolate that he might someday return to take the reins of AOL if it is ever spun off from Time Warner. In the meantime, Case has used his fabulous wealth to dabble in various real estate ventures. In 2004, for example, it was announced that he was making a $10 million investment in Exclusive Resorts, a luxury resort company based in Denver, Colorado. He also owns 50,000 acres of prime real estate in Hawaii, and it has been reported that he may develop some of that land into a luxury resort/conference center complex.

Case has three children from his marriage with Joanne Barker, whom he wed in 1985 and divorced in 1996. Two years after their divorce, he married Jean Villanueva, an executive with AOL.

Sources

Case, Steve. "My Work," undated. Available online at www.stevecase.aol.com.

Klein, Alec. *Stealing Time: Steve Case, Jerry Levin, and the Collapse of AOL Time Warner.* New York: Simon and Schuster, 2003.

McHugh, Joseph. "Web Warrior." *Forbes,* January 11, 1999.

Motavalli, John. *Bamboozled at the Revolution: How Big Media Lost Billions in the Battle for the Internet.* New York: Viking Penguin, 2002.

Munk, Nina. "Steve Case's Last Stand." *Vanity Fair,* January 2003.

"A Scapegoat Named Steve Case." *Business Week,* January 27, 2003.

"Steve Case." *Current Biography Yearbook,* 1996.

Swisher, Kara. *AOL.com: How Steve Case Beat Bill Gates, Nailed the Netheads, and Made Millions in the War for the Web.* New York: Crown, 1998.

Swisher, Kara. *There Must Be a Pony in Here Somewhere: The AOL Time Warner Debacle and the Quest for a Digital Future.* New York: Crown, 2003.

Vinton Cerf (1943-)
Computer Scientist Who Developed Early Internet Architecture

Vinton Gray Cerf was born on July 23, 1943, in New Haven, Connecticut. His parents were Vinton Thurston Cerf, an executive in the aviation industry, and Muriel (Gray) Cerf. The oldest of three sons, Cerf began to lose his hearing as a child. Hearing aids and other medical treatments eventually helped him regain much of his hearing, but he later cited his disability as a factor in his work on the Internet—a medium of communication that provides a level information playing field for non-hearing users.

During his years at Van Nuys High School in Los Angeles, Cerf loved mathematics and science fiction. He also became good friends with Steve Crocker, who would go on to make his own important contributions to the development of the Internet.

Cerf received a full academic scholarship to attend Stanford University, where he majored in mathematics. After earning a bachelor of science degree in 1965, he took a computer programming job with IBM. "There was something amazingly enticing about programming," he told Katie Hafner and Matthew Lyon in *Where Wizards Stay Up Late*. "You created your own universe and you were the master of it. The computer would do anything you programmed it to do. It was this unbelievable sandbox in which every grain of sand was under your control."

Exploring "Internetworking"

In 1966 Cerf married Sigrid L. Thorstenberg, with whom he eventually had two sons. One year later, he enrolled in the computer science program at the University of California-Los Angeles (UCLA), one of only a handful of such programs available in the United States at the time. During his computer science studies at UCLA (where he earned a master's degree in 1970 and a doctorate in 1972), he began working for the Department of Defense's

Advanced Research Projects Agency (ARPA). Cerf joined the agency at a time when the ARPANET—the forerunner of the Internet—was undergoing continuous testing and experimentation. "My job was to figure out how the system was performing and to overload it in order to find out how it would respond—whether it broke or fought back," he recalled in *Communications of the ACM.* "We managed to destroy the network on several occasions by deliberately launching too much traffic. That was part of the research—to understand how the technology would function."

By 1970 the ARPANET leadership, including Cerf, Robert Kahn, Larry Roberts, and Leonard Kleinrock, had cobbled together a modest network of computers that were electronically linked across thousands of miles. Within another two years, dozens of universities and research instituations were clamoring to link their own proprietary computer systems onto the ARPANET network. The programmers working on the ARPANET recognized that it would never reach its full potential if it remained isolated from other computer networks springing up around the world. Cerf and Kahn subsequently investigated means by which different types of computer networks might be connected through "internetworking"—a term later shortened to "Internet."

Building on the packet-switching technology developed by Kleinrock and others, Cerf and Kahn eventually came up with a plan to place "open architecture" gateways between each individual computer network and a larger "Internet." These gateways were designed to play a pivotal role in system-wide operations—translating messages between networks, breaking up information into packets, sending the packets toward their final destination, and then reassembling the packets once they got there.

In 1974 Cerf and Kahn also unveiled a set of proposed network communication rules, or protocols. Collectively dubbed TCP/IP (Transmission Control Protocol/Internet Protocol) by Cerf and Kahn, these rules addressed a host of issues to ensure that electronic information could be reliably transported across different networks.

Over the next several years Cerf and Kahn worked tirelessly, not only to refine their TCP/IP protocol, but also to convince the computer world to adopt the system. The latter was a particularly formidable task, for an assortment of different operating systems were being created by various computer makers and research organizations at the time. In July 1977, though, they increased their leverage when they successfully conducted a test that dramatically illustrated the possibilities of "internetworking." This test, which transmitted data 94,000 miles through several different types of networks by using TCP/IP protocols, grabbed the computer world's attention like nothing ever before.

"Father of the Internet"

Over the next several years, Cerf assumed such a prominent role in the development of a global computer network that he eventually became widely known as the "father of the Internet." In 1978 Cerf and Kahn split their protocol into two parts, TCP and IP, to make it less complicated and reduce the demands on gateways and individual networks. Transmission Control Protocol (TCP) became a host-to-host protocol, controlling the process of packetizing the information, while Internet Protocol (IP) addressed the routing of packets within the Internet. Over the ensuing decade, the entire ARPANET was transferred over to the TCP and IP protocols, which became the basis for network communication on the modern Internet.

During this period, Cerf emerged as the foremost advocate of utilizing TCP and IP for mainframes, minicomputers, and desktop personal computers. In 1979 he wrote *A Practical View of Communication Protocols,* which extolled the benefits of the system that he and Kahn had founded, and he championed their vision at countless computer technology conferences and other venues. "If anyone could claim credit for having worked tirelessly to promote TCP/IP, it was Cerf," wrote Hafner and Lyon in *Where Wizards Stay Up Late.* "The magic of the Internet was that its computers used a very simple communications protocol. And the magic of Vint Cerf, a colleague once remarked, was that he cajoled and negotiated and urged user communities into adopting it."

In 1981 Cerf was named lead scientist with DARPA (Defense Advanced Research Projects Agency), formerly ARPA. Working in this capacity he continued to play an essential role in the development of the Internet and Internet-related data packet and security technologies. One year later he abruptly took a job in the private sector with MCI, lured by an attractive salary package (after years of modest compensation as a government employee) and the prospect of developing an e-mail system for the Internet. The ultimate result was MCI Mail, the first commercial e-mail service to be connected to the Internet.

In 1986 Cerf joined the Corporation for National Research Initiatives (CNRI), where he took a leading role in establishing e-mail as a basic service offered by Internet providers. During the last years of the decade, meanwhile, Cerf saw clear indications that his years of labor to create and tout the Internet were coming to fruition. In 1989, for example, he attended Interop, a major trade show promoting TCP/IP-based computer networking. Unlike previous years, when the trade show was attended mainly by computer scientists, this time it was crawling with executives from major communications and technology companies across the United States and beyond. "It was an epiphany to walk into Interop and see the major money being spent on exhibitions with huge demonstrations set up," he recalled to Hafner and Lyon. "We started looking at the network statistics and realized we had a rocket on our hands."

In the early 1990s excitement about the rapidly coalescing Internet was palpable, as the introduction of a new software application called the World Wide Web made navigating the network far easier and more efficient than ever before. Taking stock of the fast-changing environment, Cerf helped found the nonprofit Internet Society in 1992 and served as its first president. He remained in that position until 1995, and later served a one-year term as chairman. He is still a member of the organization's Internet Societal Task Force, which is devoted to keeping the Internet accessible to everyone and to tracking international, national, and local policies surrounding Internet use.

In 1994 Cerf returned to MCI, which later changed its name to Worldcom. Since that time he has worked on a variety of projects concerning Internet architecture and technology for the company. In 1997 he and Robert Kahn received the U.S. National Medal of Technology from President Bill Clinton in recognition of their work founding and developing the Internet. He has also received numerous other prestigious awards, including the Alexander Graham Bell Award for contributions to improving the lives of the deaf and hearing impaired; the Computer and Communications Industries Association Industry Legend Award, the IEEE Koji Kobayashi Award, and the Library of Congress Bicentennial Living Legend medal.

Sources

Brody, Herb. "Net Cerfing." *Technology Review,* May-June 1998.

Cerf, Vint. "Commentary: Progressive Initiatives Seen for ACM." *Communications of the ACM,* October 1992.

Hafner, Katie, and Matthew Lyon. *Where Wizards Stay Up Late: The Origins of the Internet.* New York: Simon and Schuster, 1996.

Henderson, Harry. *History Makers: Pioneers of the Internet.* San Diego: Lucent Books, 2002.

David Filo (1966-)
Jerry Yang (1968 -)
Co-Founders of Yahoo! Search Engine

The partnership between Yahoo! co-founders David Filo and Jerry Yang was in some ways an unlikely one. Filo was born in Wisconsin in 1966, but grew up in Moss Bluff, Louisiana. His father, Jerry, worked as an architect, and his mother, Carol, was an accountant. Filo attended Tulane University in New Orleans, earning a bachelor's degree in computer engineering in 1988. He then went on to gain a master's degree in electrical engineering at Stanford University in Palo Alto, California. It was at Stanford that he met Yang, a fellow graduate student.

Yang was born Chih-Yuan Yang in Taiwan in November 6, 1968. He was raised by his mother, Lily, an English and drama teacher, after his father died when he was two years old. He immigrated to the United States at age 10 with his mother, grandmother, and younger brother. Upon settling in the suburbs of San Jose, California, his mother changed his name to Jerry and his younger brother's name to Ken as part of an effort to assimilate into American society.

When Yang first arrived in the United States, he spoke virtually no English. By the time he graduated from Piedmont Hills High School in 1986, however, he was class valedictorian and president of his senior class. From there he went to Stanford University in Palo Alto, California, where he obtained both bachelor's and master's degrees in electrical engineering in 1990.

A Fruitful Friendship

Yang and Filo first crossed paths at Stanford in the engineering school. In fact, they both enrolled in the same teaching program in Kyoto, Japan. It was during this program that Yang met his future wife, Akiko, a fellow Stanford student.

Upon returning to the United States, Filo and Yang became involved, as part of their doctoral work, in efforts to apply computers to the design of computer chip circuitry. But when their faculty advisor went on sabbatical, the two men instead turned much of their attention to the newly minted World Wide Web created by Tim Berners-Lee.

The Web was in its infancy at the time, but Yang and Filo nonetheless spent hours exploring various Web sites, hopscotching from hyperlink to hyperlink with abandon. As time passed, though, they became frustrated by the early Web's disorganized nature. They discovered that it was virtually impossible to find information on the Web—especially specific sites—without knowing a URL, or domain name. Determined to rectify this problem for themselves, Yang and Filo began recording the URLs of their favorite sites using a crude but effective software program of their own design. Before long, their list morphed into a Web guide of sorts that the two men decided to make available to all Internet users at Stanford. Their list, first dubbed "Jerry's Guide to the World Wide Web" and later amended to "Jerry and David's Guide to the World Wide Web," made its first appearance in early 1994.

The guide nurtured by Yang and Filo was immediately embraced by a small but growing community of Web users who were thirsty for some structure and direction in their Internet surfing activities. "And so, without really meaning to, Dave and Jerry quickly had—*ooops!*—an audience," wrote Robert Reid in *Architects of the Web:*

> And without really knowing why, they soon found themselves responding to its needs. At first they accepted, then started soliciting site submissions from their users. Then they started to expand their Guide with little featurelets, like "What's New" and "What's Cool" listings. The Guide's audience cheered every embellishment with a trickle, then a torrent of encouraging E-mails—digital applause that Jerry and Dave found to be enormously gratifying. Much of this applause came with constructive advice, so it helped shape Yahoo!'s evolution.

The Birth of Yahoo!

By the end of the summer of 1994, the guide had mushroomed into a rough guide to the Web, equipped with an abundance of new subject categories and subtopics, and it had been renamed Yahoo!, short for Yet Another Hierarchical Officious Oracle. Its popularity, meanwhile, was both stunning and exhilarating. When hits on the web site reached—then blew by—one million a day, Yang and Filo knew that they needed to take a hard look at the potential commercial applications of Yahoo! "It was amazing how many Internet startup ideas were being generated within a very close community of friends at school [at the time]," recalled Yang in *Forbes*. "And for a while, we were sitting there literally writing business plans for Internet-based business-es while on the side working on [what would become] Yahoo! ... At the time, we didn't realize the thing that we'd been working on for fun was going to be the one that succeeded. But finally we realized that if we stopped, then all those people using Yahoo! would go away and they wouldn't have anything. We felt we were offering a service that people really wanted. And that's what got us thinking about it as a business."

In the spring of 1995 Yang and Filo embarked on a quest for investors to transform Yahoo! into a serious commercial enterprise. Their efforts coincid-ed with a dizzying proliferation of Web sites and growing demand for an effi-cient means of navigating the Web. So it was not a surprise when they were able to secure a $1 million investment commitment from Mike Mortiz at Sequoia Capital, a fund that had financed several other big tech companies in their infancies. Yang and Filo then lined up Motorola executive Tim Koogle and Novell WordPerfect executive Jeffrey Mallet as chief executive officer and chief operating officer, respectively, of the company.

Yahoo! was formally launched as a commercial venture in 1995 with great optimism. As Yang told Robert Reid in *Architects of the Web*, the whole idea of starting an Internet-based business was exhilarating, akin to "being dropped off a helicopter and you're the first guy skiing down the hill. You don't know where the tree is, you don't know where the cliff is, but it's a great feeling."

A Resounding Success

As the months passed by, Yahoo!'s popularity with Web users continued to soar. Yang and Filo and the rest of the company leadership took full advantage of the business's momentum. They negotiated a business deal with Netscape so that users of the Navigator browser could link to the Yahoo! search engine with the click of an icon, and they began selling advertising space on their pages. This latter decision prompted some grousing from critics who wanted to keep the Web free of such commercial trappings. But before long, banner ads and other forms of advertisements were a ubiquitous part of the Web.

126

Other improvements to Yahoo! included deals to provide news, weather, stock quotes, and other information to users. In addition, the company was a pioneer in developing "personalized" pages (called My Yahoo!), which allowed users to customize their Yahoo! page with all the links that interested them most. Finally, the Yahoo! search engine—which was still indexed by hand while other search engines were automated—continued to expand, eventually exceeding 100,000 categories and subtopics. This service was tended by hundreds of employees who scoured the rapidly changing Web on a daily basis.

On April 12, 1996, Yahoo! made a public stock offering that set the investment world on its ear. The price of a single share of Yahoo! stock rose from a starting price of $13 to $43 before finally settling at the still-impressive price of $33. The performance was the second-largest first day gain in the history of the NASDAQ exchange. It also made Yang and Filo immensely wealthy, and boosted the value of the company to $848 million.

Over the next several years, Yang emerged as the public face of the company. "[Yang is] everything from technical visionary to chief strategist to corporate spokesman and cheerleader to Washington lobbyist to the company's conscience," one Stanford University administrator told *Fortune*. He was thus an integral part of a number of aggressive business moves initiated by Yahoo! in the late 1990s. In 1998, for example, Yahoo! joined with MCI (now WorldCom) to become an Internet service provider as well as a search engine. One year later, it acquired properties to enter the world of Internet broadcasting. In 2000 the company entered into serious negotiations to acquire eBay, a popular online auction site. The overture eventually collapsed, however, and industry analysts have since characterized the decision not to pursue eBay as a missed opportunity.

Rough Economic Waters

By 1999 Yahoo! had a market value of $70 billion, and the personal wealth of both Yang and Filo was measured in the billions as well. In early 2000 analysts estimated that the company was worth far more than such venerable corporate giants as Walt Disney Company. In 2001, though, the U.S. economy and stock market underwent a wrenching correction, as the value of legions of overvalued "dot.com" businesses went into deep downward spirals. Yahoo! suffered as well. The company's market value plummeted to $5.2 billion, and its stock price fell from more than $237 a share in January 2000 to $12 a share in November 2001.

The financial difficulties at Yahoo! resulted in the trimming of fully 12 percent of the company work force (more than 400 people) and several months of tumult in Yahoo!'s executive offices. As the company experienced a wave of high-profile departures and reassignments, it also endured months of unflattering coverage from the nation's business press.

In 2003, though, Yahoo!'s financial outlook brightened. From mid-2003 to mid-2004 the value of the company's stock more than doubled, and it remains a major force in Internet communications, commerce, and media. It continues to tout its search engine as the most popular guide to the Web in the world in terms of traffic, advertising, and households reached, claiming 232 million individual customers worldwide every month.

Yang remains a major figure at the company's headquarters in Sunnyvale, California. The most high-profile member of the company's board of directors, Yang works closely with current Yahoo! president and chief executive officer Terry Semel on corporate business strategies and planning. Yang has sold millions of shares of Yahoo! stock through blind trust arrangements in recent years, but he still controls approximately 58 million shares of Yahoo! stock.

Filo is a much less public figure, though he remains an important part of the company. Leaving promotional efforts to Yang and others, Filo works behind the scenes, directing technical operations for Yahoo!'s global network of Web properties. In 2004 Filo received a rare splash of publicity when he and Netscape co-founder Jim Clark announced donations of $30 million each to their undergraduate alma mater, Tulane University.

Sources

Angel, Karen. *Inside Yahoo! Reinvention and the Road Ahead.* New York: John Wiley, 2002.
"Inside Yahoo!" *Business Week,* May 21, 2001.
"Jerry Yang and David Filo." *Current Biography,* October 1997.
Reid, Robert H. *Architects of the Web: 1,000 Days That Built the Future of Business.* New York: John Wiley, 1997.
Schlender, Brent. "How a Virtuoso Plays the Web." *Fortune,* March 6, 2000.
Yang, Jerry. "Turn On, Type In and Drop Out." *Forbes,* December 1, 1997.

Robert Taylor (1932-)
Leading Scientist in the Development of the ARPANET

Robert William Taylor was born in 1932 in Texas. He was adopted by a Methodist minister and his wife while still an infant, and he spent the rest of his childhood in various Texas communities. He enrolled at Southern Methodist University at age 16. He served in the U.S. Navy during the Korean War, then went back to school at the University of Texas, where he eventually earned bachelor's and master's degrees.

After a brief stint coaching and teaching in Florida, Taylor moved into the field of engineering, securing employment in the aircraft industry. In 1962 he moved on to the National Atmospheric and Space Administration (NASA), where he worked as a program manager in the agency's research and technology office. During the next several years, he directed research funding to visionary computer engineers like Douglas Engelbart, who was the inventor of the computer mouse, and J.C.R. Licklider, who was the author of prescient articles on the future role of computers in modern society. In 1968 Licklider and Taylor collaborated on a research paper that opened with a bold prediction: "In a few years, men will be able to communicate more effectively through a machine than face to face."

"Father of the ARPANET"

In 1965 Taylor became deputy director of the Information Processing Techniques Office (IPTO) of the Advanced Research Projects Agency (ARPA) at the Department of Defense. A year later he was promoted to director, a position he held until late 1969.

ARPA had been created in response to the Soviet launch of the *Sputnik* satellite several years earlier. It had a mandate to pursue research into high technology areas, even if the research did not have obvious military applications. According to Taylor, this freedom was exhilarating. "We were explicitly looking for things which, if they could succeed, would really be a large step beyond what technology could then permit," he recalled in an interview with William Aspray. "We were not constrained to fund something only because of its military relevance."

As director, Taylor became convinced that ARPA's various research efforts were being badly hampered by the inability of its various mainframe computers, located hundreds of miles apart, to communicate with one another. He also recognized that much of the computer research funded by ARPA overlapped, leading to costly duplication of effort by researchers at different locations. Taylor thus decided to throw ARPA's resources behind the creation of an "ARPANET"—a system of electronic links between the ARPA research centers around the country that would ultimately create a single network. This network, the ARPANET, was the forerunner of today's Internet.

Spearheaded by Taylor, ARPA started funding projects to make the world's first interactive computer network. It contracted with Bolt Beranek and Newman (BBN) to build the system and convinced universities and research institutions to install nodes to test their ideas. With each passing month, the ARPANET coalesced into being, and in 1969 Taylor and his colleagues successfully transmitted an electronic message on the ARPANET from a node at UCLA to another mainframe at the Stanford Research Center. The ARPANET was thus born as a network for the free interchange of information between universities, research organizations, and various branches of the U.S. military.

Triumphs at PARC

Toward the end of his tenure at ARPA, Taylor went to Vietnam with the honorary rank of brigadier general as part of an effort to improve the U.S. military's war performance. In late 1969 he returned to the United States and resigned from ARPA. "The experience of Vietnam helped convince me that it was time for me to leave ARPA," he told Aspray. "In fact, we had the ARPANET up and running, so I felt like I had been there long enough."

After a year at the University of Utah, Taylor moved on to manage the Computer Systems Laboratory (CSL) at the Xerox Palo Alto Research Center (PARC). Taylor quickly instituted a creative, spontaneous work environment that proved to be fertile ground for the development of several major technological breakthroughs in personal computers and computer networking. For example, PARC was the birthplace of the Ethernet, the first local-area network (LAN), and it was the site of pioneering work in the development of graphical user interfaces (GUI). Several major technology companies also grew out of the work done at PARC in the 1970s.

Looking back on that era in 2004, Taylor explained that PARC's success was founded on the fact that the people working there "shared a dream—that computer systems could be completely redesigned and that this redesign could enable personal interactions with text, pictures, and networking for millions of individuals. The dream promised to encourage creative potential and new forms of communication…. The dream was not widely shared outside the group. The great majority of computer experts and leading computer manufacturers in the 1970s rejected these ideas as absurd. Some said, 'No one wants it; the world doesn't need so many computers. What could I possibly do with my own computer?'"

In 1983 Taylor moved to Digital Equipment Corporation, in part because of mounting frustration with Xerox's indifferent attitude toward PARC's innovative work. As director of DEC's new research center in Palo Alto, he oversaw the development of high-tech computer work stations, electronic books, and early versions of the Java programming language.

In 1996 Taylor retired to his home in Riverside, California. Three years later, he received the National Medal of Technology "for visionary leadership in the development of modern computing technology, including initiating the ARPANET project—forerunner of today's Internet." The award also acknowledged his work over the years in the development of personal computers and computer networks. In 2004 he received the Charles Stark Draper Prize, presented by the National Academy of Engineering.

Sources
Aspray, William. "Interview with Robert Taylor." Minneapolis: Charles Babbage Institute, University of Minnesota, February 28, 1989 (available online at www.cbi.umn.edu/oh/pdf.phtml?id=265).

Hafner, Katie, and Matthew Lyon. *Where Wizards Stay Up Late: The Origins of the Internet.* New York: Simon and Schuster, 1996.

Naughton, John. *A Brief History of the Future: Origins of the Internet.* London: Orion, 2000.

Softky, Marion. "Building the Internet: Bob Taylor Won the National Medal of Technology For Visionary Leadership in the Development of Modern Computing Technology," *The Almanac,* October 11, 2000 (available online at www.almanacnews.com/morgue/2000/2000_10_11.taylor.html).

Taylor, Robert. "2004 Draper Prize Acceptance Remarks." National Academy of Engineering Website (available online at www.nae.edu/NAE/awardscom.nsf/weblinks/LRAO-5X4TSP?OpenDocument).

PRIMARY SOURCES

Vinton Cerf Recalls the Early Development of the Internet

Vinton Cerf is one of the pioneers of the Internet. His involvement with computer networking begin in 1967, when he was a graduate student at the University of California-Los Angeles (UCLA) and helped test the first Interface Message Processors (IMPs) connecting the original ARPANET. He participated in the first public demonstration of the ARPANET in 1972, helped develop the TCP/IP protocols that allowed different types of networks to be connected, and led the first test of the Internet in 1977. Since then, he has watched the network he helped design and test grow at a rate that has far exceeded his expectations.

In the following excerpt from his 1993 essay "How the Internet Came to Be," Cerf describes his activities during the first 25 years in the history of the Internet. He provides an insider's perspective on some of the most important points in the technical development of the network.

The Birth of the ARPANET

My involvement began when I was at UCLA doing graduate work from 1967 to 1972. There were several people at UCLA at the time studying under Jerry Estrin, and among them was Stephen Crocker. Stephen was an old high-school friend, and when he found out that I wanted to do graduate work in computer science, he invited me to interview at UCLA.

When I started graduate school, I was originally looking at multiprocessor hardware and software. Then a Request For Proposal [RFP] came in from the Defense Advanced Research Projects Agency, DARPA [also called ARPA]. The proposal was about packet switching, and it went along with the packet-switching network that DARPA was building.

Several UCLA faculty were interested in the RFP. Leonard Kleinrock had come to UCLA from MIT [the Massachusetts Institute of Technology], and he brought with him his interest in that kind of communications environment. His thesis was titled *Communication Networks: Stochastic Flow and Delay,* and he was one of the earliest queuing theorists to examine what packet-switch networking might be like. As a result, the UCLA people proposed to DARPA to organize and run a Network Measurement Center for the ARPANET project.

This is how I wound up working at the Network Measurement Center on the implementation of a set of tools for observing the behavior of the fledgling ARPANET. The team included Stephen Crocker; Jon Postel, who has been the RFC [Request for Comments] editor from the beginning; Robert Braden, who was working at the UCLA computer center; Michael Wingfield, who built the first interface to the Internet for the Xerox Data System Sigma 7 computer, which had originally been the Scientific Data Systems (SDS) Sigma 7; and David Crocker, who became one of the central figures in electronic mail standards for the ARPANET and the Internet. Mike Wingfield built the BBN [Bolt Beranek and Newman] 1822 interface for the Sigma 7, running at 400 Kbps [kilobytes per second], which was pretty fast at the time.

Around Labor Day in 1969, BBN delivered an Interface Message Processor (IMP) to UCLA that was based on a Honeywell DDP 516, and when they turned it on, it just started running. It was hooked by 50 Kbps circuits to two other sites (SRI and UCSB) in the four-node network: UCLA, Stanford Research Institute (SRI), UC Santa Barbara (UCSB), and the University of Utah in Salt Lake City.

We used that network as our first target for studies of network congestion. It was shortly after that I met the person who had done a great deal of the architecture: Robert Kahn, who was at BBN, having gone there from MIT. Bob came out to UCLA to kick the tires of the system in the long haul environment, and we struck up a very productive collaboration. He would ask for software to do something, I would program it overnight, and we would do the tests.

One of the many interesting things about the ARPANET packet switches is that they were heavily instrumented in software, and additional programs could be installed remotely from BBN for targeted data sampling. Just as you use trigger signals with oscilloscopes, the IMPs could trigger collection of data if you got into a certain state. You could mark packets and when they went through an IMP that was programmed appropriately, the data would go to the Network Measurement Center.

There were many times when we would crash the network trying to stress it, where it exhibited behavior that Bob Kahn had expected, but that others didn't think could happen. One such behavior was reassembly lock-up. Unless you were careful about how you allocated memory, you could have a bunch of partially assembled messages but no room left to reassemble them, in which case it locked up. People didn't believe it could happen statistically, but it did. There were a bunch of cases like that.

My interest in networking was strongly influenced by my time at the Network Measurement Center at UCLA.

Meanwhile, Larry Roberts had gone from Lincoln Labs to DARPA, where he was in charge of the Information Processing Techniques Office. He was concerned that after building this network, we could do something with it. So out of UCLA came an initiative to design protocols for hosts, which Steve Crocker led.

In April 1969, Steve issued the very first Request For Comment. He observed that we were just graduate students at the time and so had no authority. So we had to find a way to document what we were doing without acting like we were imposing anything on anyone. He came up with the RFC methodology to say, "Please comment on this, and tell us what you think."

Initially, progress was sluggish in getting the protocols designed and built and deployed. By 1971 there were about nineteen nodes in the initially planned ARPANET, with thirty different university sites that ARPA was funding. Things went slowly because there was an incredible array of machines that needed interface hardware and network software. We had Tenex systems at BBN running on DEC-10s, but there were also PDP-8s, PDP-11s, IBM 360s, Multics, Honeywell … you name it. So you had to implement the protocols on each of these different architectures. In late 1971, Larry Roberts at DARPA decided that people needed serious motivation to get things going. In October 1972 there was to be an International Conference on Computer Communications, so Larry asked Bob Kahn at BBN to organize a public demonstration of the ARPANET.

It took Bob about a year to get everybody far enough along to demonstrate a bunch of applications on the ARPANET. The idea was that we would install a packet switch and a Terminal Interface Processor or TIP in the basement of the Washington Hilton Hotel, and actually let the public come in and use the ARPANET, running applications all over the U.S.

A set of people who are legendary in networking history were involved in getting that demonstration set up. Bob Metcalfe was responsible for the documentation; Ken Pogran who, with David Clark and Noel Chiappa, was instrumental in developing an early ring-based local area network and gateway, which became Proteon products, narrated the slide show; Crocker and Postel were there. Jack Haverty, who later became chief network architect of Oracle and was an MIT undergraduate, was there with a holster full of tools.

Frank Heart who led the BBN project; David Walden; Alex McKenzie; Severo Ornstein; and others from BBN who had developed the IMP and TIP. The demo was a roaring success, much to the surprise of the people at AT&T who were skeptical about whether it would work....

At the conference we formed the International Network Working Group or INWG. Stephen Crocker, who by now was at DARPA after leaving UCLA, didn't think he had time to organize the INWG, so he proposed that I do it.

I organized and chaired INWG for the first four years, at which time it was affiliated with the International Federation of Information Processing (IFIP). Alex Curran, who was president of BNR, Inc., a research laboratory of Bell Northern Research in Palo Alto, California, was the U.S. representative to IFIP Technical Committee 6. He shepherded the transformation of the INWG into the first working group of 6, working group 6.1 (IFIP WG 6.1).

In November 1972, I took up an assistant professorship post in computer science and electrical engineering at Stanford. I was one of the first Stanford acquisitions who had an interest in computer networking. Shortly after I got to Stanford, Bob Kahn told me about a project he had going with SRI International, BBN, and Collins Radio, a packet radio project. This was to get a mobile networking environment going. There was also work on a packet satellite system, which was a consequence of work that had been done at the University of Hawaii, based on the ALOHA-Net, done by Norman Abramson, Frank Kuo, and Richard Binder. It was one of the first uses of multiaccess channels. Bob Metcalfe used that idea in designing Ethernet before founding 3COM to commercialize it.

The Birth of the Internet

Bob Kahn described the packet radio and satellite systems, and the internet problem, which was to get host computers to communicate across multiple packet networks without knowing the network technology underneath. As a way of informally exploring this problem, I ran a series of seminars at Stanford attended by students and visitors.... Thinking about computer networking problems has had a powerful influence on careers; many of [the students] have gone on to make major contributions.

The very earliest work on the TCP [Transmission Control Protocol] was done at three places. The initial design work was done in my lab at Stanford. The first draft came out in the fall of 1973 for review by INWG at a meeting at

University of Sussex (September 1973). A paper by Bob Kahn and me appeared in May 1974 in *IEEE Transactions on Communications* and the first specification of the TCP protocol was published as an Internet Experiment Note in December 1974. We began doing concurrent implementations at Stanford, BBN, and University College London. So the effort at developing the Internet protocols was international from the beginning. In July 1975, the ARPANET was transferred by DARPA to the Defense Communications Agency (now the Defense Information Systems Agency) as an operational network.

About this time, military security concerns became more critical and this brought Steve Kent from BBN and Ray McFarland from DoD [U.S. Department of Defense] more deeply into the picture, along with Steve Walker, then at DARPA.

At BBN there were two other people: William Plummer and Ray Tomlinson. It was Ray who discovered that our first design lacked and needed a three-way handshake in order to distinguish the start of a new TCP connection from old random duplicate packets that showed up later from an earlier exchange. At University College London, the person in charge was Peter Kirstein. Peter had a lot of graduate and undergraduate students working in the area, using a PDP-9 machine to do the early work. They were at the far end of a satellite link to England.

Even at the beginning of this work we were faced with using satellite communications technology as well as ARPANET and packet radio. We went through four iterations of the TCP suite, the last of which came out in 1978.

The earliest demonstration of the triple network Internet was in July 1977. We had several people involved. In order to link a mobile packet radio in the Bay Area, Jim Mathis was driving a van on the San Francisco Bayshore Freeway with a packet radio system running on an LSI-11. This was connected to a gateway developed by Virginia Strazisar at BBN. Ginny was monitoring the gateway and had artificially adjusted the routing in the system. It went over the Atlantic via a point-to-point satellite link to Norway and down to London, by land line, and then back through the Atlantic Packet Satellite network (SATNET) through a Single Channel Per Carrier (SCPC) system, which had ground stations in Etam, West Virginia, Goonhilly Downs, England, and Tanum, Sweden. The German and Italian sites of SATNET hadn't been hooked in yet. Ginny was responsible for gateways from packet radio to ARPANET, and from ARPANET to SATNET. Traffic passed from the mobile unit on the Packet Radio network across the ARPANET over an internal point-to-point satellite link to University College London, and then back through the SATNET into the ARPANET again, and then across the ARPANET to the USC Information Sciences Institute to one of their DEC KA-10 (ISIC) machines. So what we were simulating was someone in a mobile battlefield environment going across a continental network, then across an intercontinental satellite network, and then back into a wireline network to a major computing resource in national headquarters. Since the Defense Department was paying for this, we were looking for demonstrations that would translate to militarily interesting scenarios. So the packets were traveling 94,000 miles round trip, as opposed to what would have been an 800-mile round trip directly on the ARPANET. We didn't lose a bit!

After that exciting demonstration, we worked very hard on finalizing the protocols. In the original design we didn't distinguish between TCP and IP; there was just TCP. In the mid-1970s, experiments were being conducted to encode voice through a packet switch, but in order to do that we had to compress the voice severely from 64 Kbps to 1800 bps. If you really worked hard to deliver every packet, to keep the voice playing out without a break, you had to put lots and lots of buffering in the system to allow sequenced reassembly after retransmissions, and you got a very unresponsive system. So Danny Cohen at ISI, who was doing a lot of work on packet voice, argued that we should find a way to deliver packets without requiring reliability. He argued it wasn't useful to retransmit a voice packet end to end. It was worse to suffer a delay of retransmission.

That line of reasoning led to separation of TCP, which guaranteed reliable delivery, from IP. So the User Datagram Protocol (UDP) was created as the user-accessible way of using IP. And that's how the voice protocols work today, via UDP.

Late in 1978 or so, the operational military started to get interested in Internet technology. In 1979 we deployed packet radio systems at Fort Bragg, and they were used in field exercises. The satellite systems were further extended to include ground stations in Italy and Germany. Internet work continued in building more implementations of TCP/IP for systems that weren't covered. While still at DARPA, I formed an Internet Configuration Control Board chaired by David Clark from MIT to assist DARPA in the planning and execution of the evolution of the TCP/IP protocol suite. This group included many of the leading researchers who contributed to the TCP/IP development and was later transformed by my successor at DARPA, Barry Leiner, into the Internet Activities Board (and is now the Internet Architecture Board of the Internet Society). In 1980, it was decided that TCP/IP would be the preferred military protocols.

In 1982 it was decided that all the systems on the ARPANET would convert over from NCP [Network Control Protocol, the existing protocol on the network] to TCP/IP. A clever enforcement mechanism was used to encourage this. We used a Link Level Protocol on the ARPANET; NCP packets used one set of one channel numbers and TCP/IP packets used another set. So it was possible to have the ARPANET turn off NCP by rejecting packets sent on those specific channel numbers. This was used to convince people that we were serious in moving from NCP to TCP/IP. In the middle of 1982, we turned off the ability of the network to transmit NCP for one day. This caused a lot of hubbub unless you happened to be running TCP/IP. It wasn't completely convincing that we were serious, so toward the middle of fall we turned off NCP for two days; then on January 1, 1983, it was turned off permanently. The guy who handled a good deal of the logistics for this was Dan Lynch; he was computer center director of USC ISI at the time. He undertook the onerous task of scheduling, planning, and testing to get people up and running on TCP/IP. As many people know, Lynch went on to found INTEROP, which has become the premier trade show for presenting Internet technology.

In the same period there was also an intense effort to get implementations to work correctly. Jon Postel engaged in a series of Bake Offs, where implementers would shoot kamikaze packets at each other. Recently, FTP [File Transfer Protocol] Software has reinstituted Bake Offs to ensure interoperability among modern vendor products.

This takes us up to 1983. 1983 to 1985 was a consolidation period. Internet protocols were being more widely implemented. In 1981, 3COM had come out with UNET, which was a UNIX TCP/IP product running on Ethernet. The significant growth in Internet products didn't come until 1985 or so, where we started seeing UNIX and local area networks joining up. DARPA had invested time and energy to get BBN to build a UNIX implementation of TCP/IP and wanted that ported into the Berkeley UNIX release in v4.2. Once that happened, vendors such as Sun started using BSD as the base of commercial products.

Steve Crocker Launches the "Request for Comments" Series

*Steve Crocker was part of a team of graduate students at the University of California-Los Ange-
les (UCLA) who were responsible for writing software to connect the university's mainframe
computer to the first Interface Message Processor (IMP). IMPs were refrigerator-sized machines
that translated information flowing between mainframes in different locations on the ARPANET,
the world's first computer network.*

*During the process of writing the IMP software, Crocker and his colleagues decided to seek input
from outside experts who were helping to develop the ARPANET. He sent out the following document, which he called Request for Comments (RFC), describing his group's findings and asking for
feedback on their ideas. Crocker's memo is widely credited with launching a process of collaborative
decision making that continues to guide the development of the modern Internet. RFC1 was the first
among thousands of RFCs that, taken together, document the technical evolution of the Internet.*

> Title: Host Software
> Author: Steve Crocker
> Installation: UCLA
> Date: 7 April 1969
> Network Working Group Request for Comment: 1
>
> CONTENTS
>
> Introduction
> I.   A Summary of the IMP Software
>   Messages
>   Links
>   IMP Transmission and Error Checking
>   Open Questions on the IMP Software
> II. Some Requirements Upon the Host-to-Host Software
>   Simple Use
>   Deep Use
>   Error Checking
> III. The Host Software
>   Establishment of a Connection
>   High Volume Transmission
>   A Summary of Primitives

From Requests for Comments 1 by Steve Crocker, April 7, 1969.

Introduction

The software for the ARPA Network exists partly in the IMPs and partly in the respective HOSTs. BB&N [Bolt Beranek and Newman, builder of the IMPs] has specified the software of the IMPs and it is the responsibility of the HOST groups to agree on HOST software.

During the summer of 1968, representatives from the initial four sites met several times to discuss the HOST software and initial experiments on the network. There emerged from these meetings a working group of three, Steve Carr from [the University of] Utah, Jeff Rulifson from SRI [Stanford Research Institute], and Steve Crocker of UCLA, who met during the fall and winter. The most recent meeting was in the last week of March in Utah. Also present was Bill Duvall of SRI who has recently started working with Jeff Rulifson.

Somewhat independently, Gerard DeLoche of UCLA has been working on the HOST-IMP interface.

I present here some of the tentative agreements reached and some of the open questions encountered. Very little of what is here is firm and reactions are expected.

I. A Summary of the IMP Software

Messages

Information is transmitted from HOST to HOST in bundles called messages. A message is any stream of not more than 8080 bits, together with its header. The header is 16 bits and contains the following information:

Destination	5 bits
Link	8 bits
Trace	1 bit
Spare	2 bits

The destination is the numerical code for the HOST to which the message should be sent. The trace bit signals the IMPs to record status information about the message and send the information back to the NMC (Network Measurement Center, i.e., UCLA). The spare bits are unused.

Links

The link field is a special device used by the IMPs to limit certain kinds of congestion. They function as follows. Between every pair of HOSTs there are 32 logical full-duplex connections over which messages may be passed in either direction. The IMPs place the restriction on these links that no HOST can send two successive messages over the same link before the IMP at the destination has sent back a special message called an RFNM (Request for Next Message). This arrangement limits the congestion one HOST can cause another if the sending HOST is attempting to send too much over one link. We note, however, that since the IMP at the destination does not have enough capacity to handle all 32 links simultaneously, the links serve their purpose only if the overload is coming from one or two links. It is necessary for the HOSTs to cooperate in this respect.

The links have the following primitive characteristics. They are always functioning and there are always 32 of them.

By "always functioning," we mean that the IMPs are always prepared to transmit another message over them. No notion of beginning or ending a conversation is contained in the IMP software. It is thus not possible to query an IMP about the state of a link (although it might be possible to query an IMP about the recent history of a link—quite a different matter!).

The other primitive characteristic of the links is that there are always 32 of them, whether they are in use or not. This means that each IMP must maintain 18 tables, each with 32 entries, regardless of the actual traffic.

The objections to the link structure notwithstanding, the links are easily programmed within the IMPs and are probably a better alternative to more complex arrangements just because of their simplicity.

IMP Transmission and Error Checking

After receiving a message from a HOST, an IMP partitions the message into one or more packets. Packets are not more than 1010 bits long and are the unit of data transmission from IMP to IMP. A 24 bit cyclic checksum is computed by the transmission hardware and is appended to an outgoing packet. The checksum is recomputed by the receiving hardware and is checked against the transmitted checksum. Packets are reassembled into messages at the destination IMP.

Open Questions on the IMP Software

1. An 8 bit field is provided for link specification, but only 32 links are provided, why?

2. The HOST is supposed to be able to send messages to its IMP. How does it do this?

3. Can a HOST, as opposed to its IMP, control RFNMs?

4. Will the IMPs perform code conversion? How is it to be controlled?

II. Some Requirements Upon the Host-to-Host Software

Simple Use

As with any new facility, there will be a period of very light usage until the community of users experiments with the network and begins to depend upon it. One of our goals must be to stimulate the immediate and easy use by a wide class of users. With this goal, it seems natural to provide the ability to use any remote HOST as if it had been dialed up from a TTY (teletype) terminal. Additionally, we would like some ability to transmit a file in a somewhat different manner perhaps than simulating a teletype.

Deep Use

One of the inherent problems in the network is the fact that all responses from a remote HOST will require on the order of a half-second or so, no matter how simple. For teletype use, we could shift to a half-duplex local-echo arrangement, but this would destroy some of the usefulness of the network. The 940 Systems, for example, have a very specialized echo.

When we consider using graphics stations or other sophisticated terminals under the control of a remote HOST, the problem becomes more severe. We must look for some method which allows us to use our most sophisticated equipment as much as possible as if we were connected directly to the remote computer.

Error Checking

The point is made by Jeff Rulifson at SRI that error checking at major software interfaces is always a good thing. He points to some experience at

147

SRI where it has saved much dispute and wasted effort. On these grounds, we would like to see some HOST to HOST checking. Besides checking the software interface, it would also check the HOST-IMP transmission hardware. (BB&N claims the HOST-IMP hardware will be as reliable as the internal registers of the HOST. We believe them, but we still want the error checking.)

III. The Host Software

Establishment of a Connection

The simplest connection we can imagine is where the local HOST acts as if it is a TTY and has dialed up the remote HOST. After some consideration of the problems of initiating and terminating such a connection, it has been decided to reserve link 0 for communication between HOST operating systems. The remaining 31 links are thus to be used as dial-up lines.

Each HOST operating system must provide to its user level programs a primitive to establish a connection with a remote HOST and a primitive to break the connection. When these primitives are invoked, the operating system must select a free link and send a message over link 0 to the remote HOST requesting a connection on the selected link. The operating system in the remote HOST must agree and send back an accepting message over link 0. In the event both HOSTs select the same link to initiate a connection and both send request messages at essentially the same time, a simple priority scheme will be invoked in which the HOST of lower priority gives way and selects another free link. One usable priority scheme is simply the ranking of HOSTS by their identification numbers. Note that both HOSTs are aware that simultaneous requests have been made, but they take complementary actions: The higher priority HOST disregards the request while the lower priority HOST sends both an acceptance and another request.

The connection so established is a TTY-like connection in the pre-log-in state. This means the remote HOST operating system will initially treat the link as if a TTY had just called up. The remote HOST will generate the same echos, expect the same log-in sequence and look for the same interrupt characters.

High Volume Transmission

Teletypes acting as terminals have two special drawbacks when we consider the transmission of a large file. The first is that some characters are special interrupt characters. The second is that special buffering techniques are often employed, and these are appropriate only for low-speed, character-at-a-time transmission.

We therefore define another class of connection to be used for the transmission of files or other large volumes of data. To initiate this class of link, user level programs at both ends of an established TTY-like link must request the establishment of a file-like connection parallel to the TTY-like link. Again the priority scheme comes into play, for the higher priority HOST sends a message over link 0 while the lower priority HOST waits for it. The user level programs are, of course, not concerned with this. Selection of the free link is done by the higher priority HOST.

File-like links are distinguished by the fact that no searching for interrupt characters takes place and buffering techniques appropriate for the higher data rates takes place.

A Summary of Primitives

Each HOST operating system must provide at least the following primitives to its users. This list is known to be necessary but not sufficient.

a) Initiate TTY-like connection with HOST x.

b) Terminate connection.

c) Send/Receive character(s) over TTY-like connection.

d) Initiate file-like connection parallel to TTY-like connection.

e) Terminate file-like connection.

f) Send/Receive over file-like connection.

Error Checking

We propose that each message carry a message number, bit count, and a checksum in its body, that is transparent to the IMP. For a checksum we suggest a 16-bit end-around-carry sum computed on 1152 bits and then circularly shifted right one bit. The right circular shift every 1152 bits is designed to catch errors in message reassembly by the IMPs.

Closer Interaction

The above described primitives suggest how a user can make simple use of a remote facility. They shed no light on how much more intricate use of the network is to be carried out. Specifically, we are concerned with the fact that at some sites a great deal of work has gone into making the computer highly responsive to a sophisticated console. Culler's consoles at UCSB [University of California at Santa Barbara] and Englebart's at SRI are at least two examples. It is clear that delays of a half-second or so for trivial echo-like responses degrade the interaction to the point of making the sophistication of the console irrelevant.

We believe that most console interaction can be divided into two parts, an essentially local, immediate and trivial part and a remote, more lengthy and significant part. As a simple example, consider a user at a console consisting of a keyboard and refreshing display screen. The program the user is talking/typing into accumulates a string of characters until a carriage return is encountered and then it processes the string. While characters are being typed, it displays the characters on the screen. When a rubout character is typed, it deletes the previous non-rubout character. If the user types H E L L O <- <- P <CR> where <- is rubout and <CR> is carriage-return, he has made nine keystrokes. If each of these keystrokes causes a message to be sent which in return invokes instructions to our display station we will quickly become bored.

A better solution would be to have the front-end of the remote program—that is the part scanning for <- and <CR>—be resident in our computer. In that case, only one five character message would be sent, i.e., H E L P <CR>, and the screen would be managed locally.

We propose to implement this solution by creating a language for console control. This language, currently named DEL, would be used by subsystem designers to specify what components are needed in a terminal and how the terminal is to respond to inputs from its keyboard, Lincoln Wand, etc. Then, as a part of the initial protocol, the remote HOST would send to the local HOST, the source language text of the program which controls the console. This program would have been by the subsystem designer in DEL, but will be compiled locally.

The specifications of DEL are under discussion. The following diagrams show the sequence of actions…. [The original paper includes diagrams that show the communication that takes place between host computers in three situations: 1. Before link establishment; 2. After link establishment and log-in; and 3. After receipt and compilation of the DEL program. The diagrams are omitted here.]

Open Questions

1. If the IMPs do code conversion, the checksum will not be correct.
2. The procedure for requesting the DEL front end is not yet specified.

IV. Initial Experiments

Experiment One

SRI is currently modifying their on-line retrieval system which will be the major software component on the Network Documentation Center so that it can be operated with model 35 teletypes. The control of the teletypes will be written in DEL. All sites will write DEL compilers and use NLS through the DEL program.

Experiment Two

SRI will write a DEL front end for full NLS, graphics included. UCLA and UTAH will use NLS with graphics.

Source: Crocker, Steve. "RFC1," April 7, 1969. Available online at http://www.faqs.org/rfcs/ rfc1.html.

A Computer Scientist Describes the Internet Worm of 1988

On November 2, 1988, the growing Internet was virtually shut down by a self-replicating program called a worm. It spread across the network within hours and infected thousands of computers, overloading them with invisible tasks and preventing operators from using them. Although it did not cause permanent damage to systems, the worm did cost millions of dollars in computing time.

The worm program was written and released by Robert Tappan Morris, Jr., a 23-year-old graduate student at Cornell University and the son of the chief scientist at the U.S. National Security Agency. Morris claimed that his program was only intended to calculate the size of the Internet, and that bugs in the program caused its replication to get out of control. Nevertheless, he became the first person indicted under the Computer Abuse and Fraud Act of 1986. Upon his conviction in 1990, Morris was sentenced to three years probation and a fine. He went on to found an Internet start-up company that was purchased by Yahoo!, and afterward he became a professor at the Massachusetts Institute of Technology (MIT).

In the following excerpt from an academic paper, Donn Seeley—a professor of computer science at the University of Utah—describes what happened during the infamous Internet Worm of 1988.

ABSTRACT

On the evening of November 2, 1988, a self-replicating program was released upon the Internet. This program (a worm) invaded VAX and Sun-3 computers running versions of Berkeley UNIX, and used their resources to attack still more computers. Within the space of hours this program had spread across the U.S., infecting hundreds or thousands of computers and making many of them unusable due to the burden of its activity. This paper provides a chronology for the outbreak and presents a detailed description of the internals of the worm, based on a C version produced by decompiling.

1. Introduction

> *There is a fine line between helping administrators protect their systems and providing a cookbook for bad guys. [Grampp and Morris, "UNIX Operating System Security"]*

November 3, 1988, is already coming to be known as Black Thursday. System administrators around the country came to work on that day and discovered

---

Excerpted with permission from "A Tour of the Worm," by Donn Seeley. Proceedings of the 1989 Winter USENIX Conference, San Diego, CA, February 1989.

that their networks of computers were laboring under a huge load. If they were able to log in and generate a system status listing, they saw what appeared to be dozens or hundreds of "shell" (command interpreter) processes. If they tried to kill the processes, they found that new processes appeared faster than they could kill them. Rebooting the computer seemed to have no effect; within minutes after starting up again, the machine was overloaded by these mysterious processes.

These systems had been invaded by a *worm*. A worm is a program that propagates itself across a network, using resources on one machine to attack other machines. (A worm is not quite the same as a *virus*, which is a program fragment that inserts itself into other programs.) The worm had taken advantage of lapses in security on systems that were running 4.2 or 4.3 BSD UNIX or derivatives like SunOS. These lapses allowed it to connect to machines across a network, bypass their login authentication, copy itself and then proceed to attack still more machines. The massive system load was generated by multitudes of worms trying to propagate the epidemic.

The Internet had never been attacked in this way before, although there had been plenty of speculation that an attack was in store. Most system administrators were unfamiliar with the concept of worms (as opposed to viruses, which are a major affliction of the PC world) and it took some time before they were able to establish what was going on and how to deal with it. This paper is intended to let people know exactly what happened and how it came about, so that they will be better prepared when it happens the next time. The behavior of the worm will be examined in detail, both to show exactly what it did and didn't do, and to show the dangers of future worms. The epigraph above is now ironic, for the author of the worm used information in that paper to attack systems. Since the information is now well known, by virtue of the fact that thousands of computers now have copies of the worm, it seems unlikely that this paper can do similar damage, but it is definitely a troubling thought. Opinions on this and other matters will be offered below.

2. Chronology

Remember, when you connect with another computer, you're connecting to every computer that computer has connected to. [Dennis Miller, on NBC's "Saturday Night Live"]

Here is the gist of a message I got: I'm sorry. [Andy Sudduth, in an anonymous posting to the TCP/IP list on behalf of the author of the worm, 11/3/88]

153

Many details of the chronology of the attack are not yet available. The following list represents dates and times that we are currently aware of. Times have all been rendered in Pacific Standard Time for convenience.

11/2:1800 (approx.)

This date and time were seen on worm files found on *prep.ai.mit.edu*, a VAX 11/750 at the MIT Artificial Intelligence Laboratory. The files were removed later, and the precise time was lost. System logging on *prep* had been broken for two weeks. The system doesn't run accounting and the disks aren't backed up to tape: a perfect target. A number of "tourist" users (individuals using public accounts) were reported to be active that evening. These users would have appeared in the session logging, but see below.

11/2:1824

First known West Coast infection: *rand.org* at Rand Corp. in Santa Monica.

11/2:1904

csgw.berkeley.edu is infected. This machine is a major network gateway at UC Berkeley. Mike Karels and Phil Lapsley discover the infection shortly afterward.

11/2:1954

mimsy.umd.edu is attacked through its *finger* server. This machine is at the University of Maryland College Park Computer Science Department.

11/2: 2000 (approx.)

Suns at the MIT AI Lab are attacked.

11/2: 2028

First *sendmail* attack on *mimsy*.

11/2: 2040

Berkeley staff figure out the *sendmail* and *rsh* attacks, notice *telnet* and *finger* peculiarities, and start shutting these services off.

11/2: 2049

cs.utah.edu is infected. This VAX 8600 is the central Computer Science Department machine at the University of Utah. The next several entries follow documented events at Utah and are representative of other infections around the country.

11/2: 2109

First *sendmail* attack at *cs.utah.edu.*

11/2: 2121

The load average on *cs.utah.edu* reaches 5. The "load average" is a system-generated value that represents the average number of jobs in the run queue over the last minute; a load of 5 on a VAX 8600 noticeably degrades response times, while a load over 20 is a drastic degradation. At 9 PM, the load is typically between 0.5 and 2.

11/2: 2141

The load average on *cs.utah.edu* reaches 7.

11/2: 2201

The load average on *cs.utah.edu* reaches 16.

11/2: 2206

The maximum number of distinct runnable processes (100) is reached on *cs.utah.edu;* the system is unusable.

11/2: 2220

Jeff Forys at Utah kills off worms on *cs.utah.edu.* Utah Sun clusters are infected.

11/2: 2241

Re-infestation causes the load average to reach 27 on *cs.utah.edu.*

11/2: 2249

Forys shuts down *cs.utah.edu.*

11/3: 2321

Re-infestation causes the load average to reach 37 on *cs.utah.edu,* despite continuous efforts by Forys to kill worms.

11/2: 2328

Peter Yee at NASA Ames Research Center posts a warning to the TCP-IP mailing list: "We are currently under attack from an Internet VIRUS. It has hit UC Berkeley, UC San Diego, Lawrence Livermore, Stanford, and NASA Ames." He suggests turning off *telnet*, *ftp*, *finger*, *rsh* and SMTP services. He does not mention *rexec*. Yee is actually at Berkeley working with Keith Bostic, Mike Karels and Phil Lapsley.

11/3: 0034

> At another's prompting, Andy Sudduth of Harvard anonymously posts a
> warning to the TCP-IP list: "There may be a virus loose on the internet."
> This is the first message that (briefly) describes how the *finger* attack works,
> describes how to defeat the SMTP attack by rebuilding *sendmail,* and explic-
> itly mentions the *rexec* attack. Unfortunately Sudduth's message is blocked
> at relay.cs.net while that gateway is shut down to combat the worm, and it
> does not get delivered for almost two days. Sudduth acknowledges author-
> ship of the message in a subsequent message to TCP-IP on Nov. 5.

11/3: 0254

> Keith Bostic sends a fix for *sendmail* to the newsgroup comp.bugs.
> 4bsd.ucb-fixes and to the TCP-IP mailing list. These fixes (and later
> ones) are also mailed directly to important system administrators
> around the country.

11/3: early morning

> The wtmp session log is mysteriously removed on prep.ai.mit.edu.

11/3: 0507

> Edward Wang at Berkeley figures out and reports the *finger* attack, but
> his message doesn't come to Mike Karels' attention for 12 hours.

11/3: 0900

> The annual Berkeley Unix Workshop commences at UC Berkeley. 40 or
> so important system administrators and backers are in town to attend,
> while disaster erupts at home. Several people who had planned to fly in
> on Thursday morning are trapped by the crisis. Keith Bostic spends
> much of the day on the phone at the Computer Systems Research Group
> offices answering calls from panicked system administrators from
> around the country.

11/3: 1500 (approx.)

> The team at MIT Athena calls Berkeley with an example of how the *fin-
> ger* server bug works.

11/3: 1626

> Dave Pare arrives at Berkeley CSRG offices; disassembly and decompil-
> ing start shortly afterward using Pare's special tools.

11/3: 1800 (approx.)

The Berkeley group sends out for calzones. People arrive and leave; the offices are crowded, there's plenty of excitement. Parallel work is in progress at MIT Athena; the two groups swap code.

11/3: 1918

Keith Bostic posts a fix for the *finger* server.

11/4: 0600

Members of the Berkeley team, with the worm almost completely disassembled and largely decompiled, finally take off for a couple hours' sleep before returning to the workshop.

11/4: 1236

Theodore Ts'o of Project Athena at MIT publicly announces that MIT and Berkeley have completely disassembled the worm.

11/4:1700 (approx.)

A short presentation on the worm is made at the end of the Berkeley UNIX Workshop.

11/8:

National Computer Security Center meeting to discuss the worm. There are about 50 attendees.

11/11: 0038

Fully decompiled and commented worm source is installed at Berkeley.

3. Overview

What exactly did the worm do that led it to cause an epidemic? The worm consists of a 99-line bootstrap program written in the C language, plus a large relocatable object file that comes in VAX and Sun-3 flavors. Internal evidence showed that the object file was generated from C sources, so it was natural to decompile the binary machine language into C; we now have over 3200 lines of commented C code which recompiles and is mostly complete. We shall start the tour of the worm with a quick overview of the basic goals of the worm, followed by discussion in depth of the worm's various behaviors as revealed by decompilation.

The activities of the worm break down into the categories of attack and defense. Attack consists of locating hosts (and accounts) to penetrate, then exploiting security holes on remote systems to pass across a copy of the worm and run it. The worm obtains host addresses by examining the system tables */etc/hosts.equiv* and */.rhosts,* user files like *.forward* and *.rhosts,* dynamic routing information produced by the netstat program, and finally randomly generated host addresses on local networks. It ranks these by order of preference, trying a file like */etc/hosts.equiv* first because it contains names of local machines that are likely to permit unauthenticated connections. Penetration of a remote system can be accomplished in any of three ways. The worm can take advantage of a bug in the *finger* server that allows it to download code in place of a *finger* request and trick the server into executing it. The worm can use a "trap door" in the *sendmail* SMTP mail service, exercising a bug in the debugging code that allows it to execute a command interpreter and download code across a mail connection. If the worm can penetrate a local account by guessing its password, it can use the *rexec* and *rsh* remote command interpreter services to attack hosts that share that account. In each case the worm arranges to get a remote command interpreter which it can use to copy over, compile and execute the 99-line bootstrap. The bootstrap sets up its own network connection with the local worm and copies over the other files it needs, and using these pieces a remote worm is built and the infection procedure starts over again.

Defense tactics fall into three categories: preventing the detection of intrusion, inhibiting the analysis of the program, and authenticating other worms. The worm's simplest means of hiding itself is to change its name. When it starts up, it clears its argument list and sets its zeroth argument to *sh,* allowing it to masquerade as an innocuous command interpreter. It uses *fork()* to change its process I.D., never staying too long at one I.D. These two tactics are intended to disguise the worm's presence on system status listings. The worm tries to leave as little trash lying around as it can, so at start-up it reads all its support files into memory and deletes the tell-tale filesystem copies. It turns off the generation of *core* files, so if the worm makes a mistake, it doesn't leave evidence behind in the form of *core* dumps. The latter tactic is also designed to block analysis of the program—it prevents an administrator from sending a software signal to the worm to force it to dump a *core* file. There are other ways to get a *core* file, however, so the worm carefully alters character data in memory to prevent it from being extracted easily. Copies of disk files are encoded by repeatedly exclusive-or'ing a ten-byte code sequence; static strings are encoded byte-by-byte by exclusive-or'ing with the hexadecimal value 81, except for a private word list which is encoded with hexadecimal 80 instead. If the worm's files are somehow captured before the worm can delete them, the object files have been loaded in such a way as to remove most non-essential symbol table entries, making it harder to guess at the purposes of worm routines from their names. The worm also makes a trivial effort to stop other programs from taking advantage of its communications; in theory a well-prepared site could prevent infection by sending messages to ports that the worm was listening on, so the worm is careful to test connections using a short exchange of random "magic numbers."

When studying a tricky program like this, it's just as important to establish what the program does not do as what it does do. The worm does not delete a system's files: it only removes files that it created in the process of bootstrapping. The program does not attempt to incapacitate a system by deleting important files, or indeed any files. It does not remove log files or otherwise interfere with normal operation other than by consuming system resources. The worm does not modify existing files: it is not a virus. The worm propagates by copying itself and compiling itself on each system; it does not modify other programs to do its work for it. Due to its method of infection, it can't count on sufficient privileges to be able to modify programs. The worm does not install trojan horses: its method of attack is strictly active, it never waits for a user to trip over a trap. Part of the reason for this is that the worm can't afford to waste time waiting for trojan horses—it must reproduce before it is discovered. Finally, the worm does not record or transmit decrypted passwords: except for its own static list of favorite passwords, the worm does not propagate cracked passwords on to new worms nor does it transmit them back to some home base. This is not to say that the accounts that the worm penetrated are secure merely because the worm did not tell anyone what their passwords were, of course—if the worm can guess an account's password, certainly others can too. The worm does not try to capture superuser privileges: while it does try to break into accounts, it doesn't depend on having particular privileges to propagate, and never makes special use of such privileges if it somehow gets them. The worm does not propagate over uucp or X.25 or DECNET or BITNET: it specifically requires TCP/IP. The worm does not infect System V systems unless they have been modified to use Berkeley network programs like *sendmail*, *fingerd* and *rexec*....

[Section 4 of this document, which is omitted here, contains a detailed examination of the internal, technical workings of the worm program.]

5. Opinions

The act of breaking into a computer system has to have the same social stigma as breaking into a neighbor's house. It should not matter that the neighbor's door is unlocked. [Ken Thompson, 1983 Turing Award Lecture]

[Creators of viruses are] stealing a car for the purpose of joyriding. [R. H. Morris, in 1983 Capitol Hill testimony, cited in the New York Times 11/11/88]

I don't propose to offer definitive statements on the morality of the worm's author, the ethics of publishing security information or the security needs of the UNIX computing community, since people better (and less) qualified than I are still copiously flaming on these topics in the various network newsgroups and mailing lists. For the sake of the mythical ordinary system administrator who might have been confused by all the information and misinformation, I will try to answer a few of the most relevant questions in a narrow but useful way.

Did the worm cause damage? The worm did not destroy files, intercept private mail, reveal passwords, corrupt databases or plant trojan horses. It did compete for CPU time with, and eventually overwhelm, ordinary user processes. It used up limited system resources such as the open file table and the process text table, causing user processes to fail for lack of same. It caused some machines to crash by operating them close to the limits of their capacity, exercising bugs that do not appear under normal loads. It forced administrators to perform one or more reboots to clear worms from the system, terminating user sessions and long-running jobs. It forced administrators to shut down network gateways, including gateways between important nation-wide research networks, in an effort to isolate the worm; this led to delays of up to several days in the exchange of electronic mail, causing some projects to miss deadlines and others to lose valuable research time. It made systems staff across the country drop their ongoing hacks and work 24-hour days trying to corner and kill worms. It caused members of management in at least one institution to become so frightened that they scrubbed all the disks at their facility that were online at the time of the infection, and limited reloading of files to data that was verifiably unmodified by a foreign agent. It caused bandwidth through gateways that were still running after the infection started to become

160

substantially degraded—the gateways were using much of their capacity just shipping the worm from one network to another. It penetrated user accounts and caused it to appear that a given user was disturbing a system when in fact they were not responsible. It's true that the worm could have been far more harmful that it actually turned out to be: in the last few weeks, several security bugs have come to light which the worm could have used to thoroughly destroy a system. Perhaps we should be grateful that we escaped incredibly awful consequences, and perhaps we should also be grateful that we have learned so much about the weaknesses in our systems' defenses, but I think we should share our gratefulness with someone other than the worm's author.

Was the worm malicious? Some people have suggested that the worm was an innocent experiment that got out of hand, and that it was never intended to spread so fast or so widely. We can find evidence in the worm to support and to contradict this hypothesis. There are a number of bugs in the worm that appear to be the result of hasty or careless programming. For example, in the worm's if *init()* routine, there is a call to the block zero function *bzero()* that incorrectly uses the block itself rather than the block's address as an argument. It's also possible that a bug was responsible for the ineffectiveness of the population control measures used by the worm. This could be seen as evidence that a development version of the worm "got loose" accidentally, and perhaps the author originally intended to test the final version under controlled conditions, in an environment from which it would not escape. On the other hand, there is considerable evidence that the worm was designed to reproduce quickly and spread itself over great distances. It can be argued that the population-control hacks in the worm are anemic by design: they are a compromise between spreading the worm as quickly as possible and raising the load enough to be detected and defeated. A worm will exist for a substantial amount of time and will perform a substantial amount of work even if it loses the roll of the (imaginary) dice; moreover, 1 in 7 worms become immortal and can't be killed by dice rolls. There is ample evidence that the worm was designed to hamper efforts to stop it even after it was identified and captured. It certainly succeeded in this, since it took almost a day before the last mode of infection (the *finger* server) was identified, analyzed and reported widely; the worm was very successful in propagating itself during this time even on systems which had fixed the *sendmail debug* problem and had turned off *rexec*. Finally, there is evidence that the worm's author deliberately introduced the worm to a foreign site that was left open and welcome to casual outside users, rather ungraciously abusing this hospitality. He apparently further abused this trust by deleting a log file that might have revealed information that could link his home site with the infection. I think the innocence lies in the research community rather than with the worm's author.

Will publication of worm details further harm security? In a sense, the worm itself has solved that problem: it has published itself by sending copies to hundreds or thousands of machines around the world. Of course a bad guy who wants to use the worm's tricks would have to go through the same effort that we went through in order to understand the program, but then it only took us a week to completely decompile the program, so while it takes fortitude to hack the worm, it clearly is not greatly difficult for a decent programmer. One of the worm's most effective tricks was advertised when it entered—the bulk of the *sendmail* hack is visible in the log file, and a few minutes' work with the sources will reveal the rest of the trick. The worm's fast password algorithm could be useful to the bad guys, but at least two other faster implementations have been available for a year or more, so it isn't very secret, or even very original. Finally, the details of the worm have been well enough sketched out on various newsgroups and mailing lists that the principal hacks are common knowledge. I think it's more important that we understand what happened, so that we can make it less likely to happen again, than that we spend time in a futile effort to cover up the issue from everyone but the bad guys. Fixes for both source and binary distributions are widely available, and anyone who runs a system with these vulnerabilities needs to look into these fixes immediately, if they haven't done so already.

6. Conclusion

> *It has raised the public awareness to a considerable degree.*
> [*R. H. Morris, quoted in the* New York Times *11/5/88]*

This quote is one of the understatements of the year. The worm story was on the front page of the *New York Times* and other newspapers for days. It was the subject of television and radio features. Even the "Bloom County" comic strip poked fun at it.

Our community has never before been in the limelight in this way, and judging by the response, it has scared us. I won't offer any fancy platitudes about how the experience is going to change us, but I will say that I think these issues have been ignored for much longer than was safe, and I feel that a better understanding of the crisis just past will help us cope better with the next one. Let's hope we're as lucky next time as we were this time.

Source: Seeley, Donn. "A Tour of the Worm," 1988. Available online at http://www.utdallas. edu/ ~edsha/security/internet-worm-tour.pdf.

The First World Wide Web Page with Hypertext Links

Tim Berners-Lee first proposed the combination of software programs and networking protocols known as the World Wide Web in 1989. It was first implemented the following year, and an improved version was made available to the public in 1991. One of the main features of the Web is hypertext, which provides a method for creating links between documents. On a computer screen, hypertext links appear as highlighted words, pictures, or icons. By clicking on a highlighted link, users can instantly jump to related information.

The historic document that appears below is a copy of the first Web page Berners-Lee created to demonstrate the power of hypertext links. The text describes his invention—the World Wide Web—and the embedded links transport users to supporting documents. In this version of the document, the original hypertext links are underlined.

World Wide Web

The WorldWideWeb (W3) is a wide-area <u>hypermedia</u> information retrieval initiative aiming to give universal access to a large universe of documents.

Everything there is online about W3 is linked directly or indirectly to this document, including an <u>executive summary</u> of the project, <u>Mailing lists,</u> <u>Policy</u>, November's <u>W3 news,</u> Frequently Asked Questions.

<u>What's out there?</u>

Pointers to the world's online information, <u>subjects</u>, <u>W3 servers</u>, etc.

<u>Help</u>

on the browser you are using.

<u>Software Products</u>

A list of W3 project components and their current state. (e.g. <u>Line Mode</u>, X11 <u>Viola</u>, <u>NeXTStep</u>, <u>Servers</u>, <u>Tools,</u> Mail robot, Library)

<u>Technical</u>

Details of protocols, formats, program internals etc.

<u>Bibliography</u>

Paper documentation on W3 and references.

<u>People</u>

A list of some people involved in the project.

<u>History</u>

A summary of the history of the project.

<u>How can I help</u>?

If you would like to support the web.

<u>Getting code</u>

Getting the code by <u>anonymous FTP</u>, etc.

Source: Berners-Lee, Tim. "World Wide Web." Available online at http://www.w3.org/History/
19921 103-hypertext/hypertext/www/The Project.html.

Tim Berners-Lee Remembers Inventing the World Wide Web

In 1999 Tim Berners-Lee published a book chronicling his invention of the World Wide Web—a combination of software programs and networking protocols that turned the formerly disorganized Internet into a weblike, interconnected "global information space." In this excerpt from his book Weaving the Web, *Berners-Lee explains how the idea behind the Web grew out of a variety of influences over a number of years. Specifically, he discusses his effort to arrange ideas in a weblike pattern rather than in a linear, hierarchical way. He also shares his vision for the future of the technology.*

When I first began tinkering with a software program that eventually gave rise to the idea of the World Wide Web, I named it Enquire, short for *Enquire Within upon Everything,* a musty old book of Victorian advice I noticed as a child in my parents' house outside London. With its title suggestive of magic, the book served as a portal to a world of information, everything from how to remove clothing stains to tips on investing money. Not a perfect analogy for the Web, but a primitive starting point.

What that first bit of Enquire code led me to was something much larger, a vision encompassing the decentralized, organic growth of ideas, technology, and society. The vision I have for the Web is about anything being potentially connected with anything. It is a vision that provides us with new freedom, and allows us to grow faster than we ever could when we were fettered by the hierarchical classification systems into which we bound ourselves. It leaves the entirety of our previous ways of working as just one tool among many. It leaves our previous fears for the future as one set among many. And it brings the workings of society closer to the workings of our minds.

Unlike *Enquire Within upon Everything,* the Web that I have tried to foster is not merely a vein of information to be mined, nor is it just a reference or research tool. Despite the fact that the ubiquitous *www* and *.com* now fuel electronic commerce and stock markets all over the world, this is a large, but just one, part of the Web. Buying books from Amazon.com and stocks from E-trade is not all there is to the Web. Neither is the Web some idealized space where we must remove our shoes, eat only fallen fruit, and eschew commercialization.

Excerpt from Chapter One, pages 1-5 from *Weaving the Web* by Tim Berners-Lee. Copyright © 1999 by Tim Berners-Lee. Reprinted with permission of HarperCollins Publishers Inc.

The irony is that in all its various guises—commerce, research, and surfing—the Web is already so much a part of our lives that familiarity has clouded our perception of the Web itself. To understand the Web in the broadest and deepest sense, to fully partake of the vision that I and my colleagues share, one must understand how the Web came to be.

The story of how the Web was created has been told in various books and magazines. Many accounts I've read have been distorted or just plain wrong. The Web resulted from many influences on my mind, half-formed thoughts, disparate conversations, and seemingly disconnected experiments. I pieced it together as I pursued my regular work and personal life. I articulated the vision, wrote the first Web programs, and came up with the now pervasive acronyms URL (then UDI), HTTP, HTML, and, of course, World Wide Web. But many other people, most of them unknown, contributed essential ingredients, in much the same almost random fashion. A group of individuals holding a common dream and working together at a distance brought about a great change.

My telling of the real story will show how the Web's evolution and its essence are inextricably linked. Only by understanding the Web at this deeper level will people ever truly grasp what its full potential can be.

Journalists have always asked me what the crucial idea was, or what the singular event was, that allowed the Web to exist one day when it hadn't the day before. They are frustrated when I tell them there was no "Eureka!" moment. It was not like the legendary apple falling on Newton's head to demonstrate the concept of gravity. Inventing the World Wide Web involved my growing realization that there was a power in arranging ideas in an unconstrained, weblike way. And that awareness came to me through precisely that kind of process. The Web arose as the answer to an open challenge, through the swirling together of influences, ideas, and realizations from many sides, until, by the wondrous offices of the human mind, a new concept jelled. It was a process of accretion, not the linear solving of one well-defined problem after another.

I am the son of mathematicians. My mother and father were part of the team that programmed the world's first commercial, stored-program computer, the Manchester University "Mark I," which was sold by Ferranti Ltd. in the early 1950s. They were full of excitement over the idea that, in principle, a person could program a computer to do most anything. They also knew, however, that computers were good at logical organizing and processing, but

167

not random associations. A computer typically keeps information in rigid hierarchies and matrices, whereas the human mind has the special ability to link random bits of data. When I smell coffee, strong and stale, I may find myself again in a small room over a coffeehouse in Oxford. My brain makes a link, and instantly transports me there.

One day when I came home from high school, I found my father working on a speech for Basil de Ferranti. He was reading books on the brain, looking for clues about how to make a computer intuitive, able to complete connections as the brain did. We discussed the point; then my father went on to his speech and I went on to my homework. But the idea stayed with me that computers could become much more powerful if they could be programmed to link otherwise unconnected information.

This challenge stayed on my mind throughout my studies at Queen's College at Oxford University, where I graduated in 1976 with a degree in physics. It remained in the background when I built my own computer with an early microprocessor, an old television, and a soldering iron, as well as during the few years I spent as a software engineer with Plessey Telecommunications and with D.G. Nash Ltd.

Then, in 1980, I took a brief software consulting job with CERN, the famous European Particle Physics Laboratory in Geneva. That's where I wrote Enquire, my first weblike program. I wrote it in my spare time and for my personal use, and for no loftier reason than to help me remember the connections among the various people, computers, and projects at the lab. Still, the larger vision had taken firm root in my consciousness.

Suppose all the information stored on computers everywhere were linked, I thought. *Suppose I could program my computer to create a space in which anything could be linked to anything.* All the bits of information in every computer at CERN, and on the planet, would be available to me and to anyone else. There would be a single, global information space.

Once a bit of information in that space was labeled with an address, I could tell my computer to get it. By being able to reference anything with equal ease, a computer could represent associations between things that might seem unrelated but somehow did, in fact, share a relationship. A web of information would form.

168

Computers might not find the solutions to our problems, but they would be able to do the bulk of the legwork required, assisting our human minds in intuitively finding ways through the maze. The added excitement was that computers could also follow and analyze the tentative connective relationships that defined much of society's workings, unveiling entirely new ways to see our world. A system able to do that would be a fantastic thing for managers, for social scientists, and, ultimately, for everyone.

Source: Berners-Lee, Tim, with Mark Fischetti. *Weaving the Web: The Original Design and Ultimate Destiny of the World Wide Web by Its Inventor.* New York: HarperCollins, 1999.

A Librarian Shares the Joy of "Surfing" the Internet

Jean Armour Polly—a librarian, author, and Web site reviewer—is widely credited with coining the term "surfing" to describe the process of exploring and searching for information on the Internet. The term first appeared in the title of her article "Surfing the Internet: An Introduction," which was published in Wilson Library Bulletin *in June 1992. In this excerpt, Polly shares her enjoyment of the valuable new resource with her fellow librarians.*

Today I'll travel to Minnesota, Texas, California, Cleveland, New Zealand, Sweden, and England. I'm not frantically packing, and I won't pick up any frequent flyer mileage. In fact, I'm sipping cocoa at my Macintosh. My trips will be electronic, using the computer on my desk, communications software, a modem, and a standard phone line.

I'll be using the Internet, the global network of computers and their interconnections, which lets me skip like a stone across oceans and continents and control computers at remote sites. I haven't "visited" Antarctica yet, but it is only a matter of time before a host computer becomes available there!

This short, non-technical article is an introduction to Internet communications and how librarians and libraries can benefit from net connectivity. Following will be descriptions of electronic mail, discussion lists, electronic journals and texts, and resources available to those willing to explore....

What's Out There Anyway?

Until you use a radio receiver, you are unaware of the wealth of programming, music, and information otherwise invisible to you.

Computer networks are much the same. About one million people worldwide use the Internet daily. Information packet traffic rises by 15 percent each month.

About 727,000 host computers are connected, according to a January 1992 report (Network Working Group Request for Comments: 1296) by Mark K. Lottor.

So, what's all the excitement about? What's zipping around in that fiber and cable and ether, anyway?

Reprinted with permission from "Surfing the Internet: An Introduction," by Jean Armour Polly, *Wilson Library Bulletin*, June 1992.

On my electronic adventure I browsed the online catalog at the University Library in Liverpool, England, leaving some "hi there from Liverpool, New York" mail for the librarian. I downloaded some new Macintosh anti-virus software from Stanford's SUMEX archive. Then I checked a few databases for information needed for this article, and scanned today's news stories. I looked at the weather forecast for here in the East and for the San Francisco Bay area, forwarding that information to a friend in San Jose who would read it when he woke up. The Internet never closes!

After that I read some electronic mail from other librarians in Israel, Korea, England, Australia, and all over the U.S. We're exchanging information about how to keep viruses off public computers, how to network CD ROMs, and how to re-ink inkjet printer cartridges, among other things.

I monitor about twelve discussion groups. Mail sent to the group address is distributed to all other "subscribers." It's similar to a round-robin discussion. These are known variously as mailing lists, discussion groups, reflectors, aliases, or listservs, depending on what type they are and how they are driven. Subscriptions are free.

One of these groups allows children and young adults all over the world to communicate with each other. Kids from Cupertino to Moscow are talking about their lives, pets, families, hopes, and dreams. It's interesting to see that Nintendo is a universal language!

Teachers exchange lesson plans and bibliographies in another group, and schools participate in projects like the global market basket survey. For this project, students researched what foods a typical family of four would buy and prepare over one week's time. Their results were posted to the global project area, where they could be compared with reports from kids all over North and South America, India, Scandinavia, and Asia. It opened up discussions of dietary laws, staple foods, and cultural differences.

Other lists explore the worlds of library administration, reference, mystery readers, romance readers, bird-watcher hotlines, cat enthusiasts, X-Soviet Union watchers, packet radio techies, and thousands more. There is even a list to announce the creation of new lists!

The Power of the Net

A net connection in a school is like having multiple foreign exchange students in the classroom all the time. It promotes active, participatory learning.

Participating in a discussion group is like being at an ongoing library conference. All the experts are Out There, waiting to be asked. Want to buy a CD ROM drive? Send one query and "ask" the 3,000 folks on PACS-L (Public Access Computer Systems list) for advice. In a few hours you'll have personal testimonies on the pros and cons of various hardware configurations.

Want to see if any libraries are doing anything with Total Quality Management? Ask the members of LIBADMIN and you'll have offers of reports, studies, personal experiences, and more.

How do you cope with budget cuts: personnel layoffs or materials? Again, LIBADMIN use allows shared advice.

Here is one story about the power of the net. At Christmas, an electronic plea came from Ireland. "My daughter believes in Santa Claus," it began. "And although the My Little Pony 'Megan & Sundance' set has not been made in three years, she believes Santa will prevail and she will find one under her tree."

Mom, a university professor, had called the manufacturer in the U.S., but none were available. "Check around," they said, "maybe some yet stand on store shelves." So, Mom sent the call out to the net.

Many readers began a global search for the wily Pony as part of their own holiday shopping forays. Soon, another message came from Dublin. It seemed that a reader of the original message had a father who was a high-ranking executive in the toy company, and he had managed to acquire said pony where others had failed! It was duly shipped in time to save Santa's reputation.

Part of the library's mission is to help remove barriers to accessing information, and part of this is removing barriers between people. One of the most interesting things about telecommunications is that it is the Great Equalizer. It lets all kinds of computers and humans talk to each other.

The old barriers of sexism, ageism, and racism are not present, since you can't see the person to whom you're "speaking." You get to know the person without preconceived notions about what you THINK he is going to say, based on visual prejudices you may have, no matter how innocent.

Not that electronic mail is always a harmonic convergence of like souls adrift in the cyberspace cosmos: of course there are arguments and tirades (called "flames"). Sometimes you get so used to seeing a frequent poster's electronic signature that you know what he's going to say before he says it!

Smileys

One problem with written communication is that remarks meant to be humorous are often lost. Without the visual body-language clues, some messages may be misinterpreted. So a visual shorthand known as "smileys" has been developed. There are a hundred or more variations on this theme— :-) That's a little smiley face. Look at it sideways.

What a range of emotions you can show using only keyboard characters. Besides the smiley face above, you can have :-(if you're sad, or :-< if you're REALLY upset! ;-) is one way of showing a wink. Folks wearing glasses might look like this online: %^).

But for the most part, the electronic community is willing to help others. Telecommunications helps us overcome what has been called the tyranny of distance. We DO have a global village.

Source: Polly, Jean Armour. "Surfing the Internet: An Introduction." *Wilson Library Bulletin,* June 1992. Available online at http://www.netmom.com/index.php?module=ContentExpress&func=print&ceid=5.

confront yourselves. In our world, all the sentiments and expressions of humanity, from the debasing to the angelic, are parts of a seamless whole, the global conversation of bits. We cannot separate the air that chokes from the air upon which wings beat.

In China, Germany, France, Russia, Singapore, Italy, and the United States, you are trying to ward off the virus of liberty by erecting guard posts at the frontiers of Cyberspace. These may keep out the contagion for a small time, but they will not work in a world that will soon be blanketed in bit-bearing media.

Your increasingly obsolete information industries would perpetuate themselves by proposing laws, in America and elsewhere, that claim to own speech itself throughout the world. These laws would declare ideas to be another industrial product, no more noble than pig iron. In our world, whatever the human mind may create can be reproduced and distributed infinitely at no cost. The global conveyance of thought no longer requires your factories to accomplish.

These increasingly hostile and colonial measures place us in the same position as those previous lovers of freedom and self-determination who had to reject the authorities of distant, uninformed powers. We must declare our virtual selves immune to your sovereignty, even as we continue to consent to your rule over our bodies. We will spread ourselves across the Planet so that no one can arrest our thoughts.

We will create a civilization of the Mind in Cyberspace. May it be more humane and fair than the world your governments have made before.

Davos, Switzerland

February 8, 1996

Source: Barlow, John Perry. "Declaration of Independence for Cyberspace," February 8, 1996. Available online at http://www.eff.org/~barlow/Declaration-Final.html.

Bill Gates Discusses the Internet's Potential Impact on Education

Microsoft founder Bill Gates has emerged as one of the leading figures in the drive to spread Internet access to people across the United States and around the world. He believes that the Internet offers many advantages, particularly in the area of education. In this excerpt from a 1999 speech at the New York Institute of Technology, Gates describes some of the potential uses of Internet technology in education. He also suggests that the Internet will be such an indispensable tool for today's youth that they should be called "Generation I."

This is truly an exciting era. The major advances to be made in technology are transforming the way we do business. It's allowing us to work in more efficient ways and to reach out for new ideas and new products that wouldn't have been possible before. The news is full every week of new start-up companies that are taking advantage of these advances. But today I want to focus on what I think is really the most exciting use of the new technology. And that is to use it as an educational tool for the new generation. There's a lot that we need to do to achieve the potential here for bringing this tool into the classrooms. In fact, if we look at it in a generational time frame, we can say that the kids who have been born just recently, they will grow up with the Internet as a fact of life for them from the very beginning. If we give them the right opportunities, they'll show us how to take full advantage of what can be done with all these advances.

The PC era started 25 years ago. That's when the first microprocessor chip came out from Intel. That's when Microsoft was founded by myself and Paul Allen. And we had a vision then that the combination of microprocessor technology along with great software from thousands of companies would create a tool that would be valuable for everyone. Our vision was a computer on every desk and in every home. And during the last 25 years, we've made incredible progress towards that dream. Today, over half of U.S. households have a personal computer. And in the workplace it's become a standard tool for creating documents and communicating.

Now, a key element of this is taking those PCs and hooking them together using the standards of the Internet. If we look at the statistics there, we have further to go. Only about 30 percent of kids at home today have both a PC and Internet access. Now, that's up very dramatically from just a few years ago, so the trend is in the right direction, but 70 percent of kids don't have that access today. We're quite certain these numbers will continue to grow as the cost of the hardware and the cost of the communications comes down, and also [as] it's viewed as more and more of a vital tool. The things that are really driving this phenomena are that more and more of the world's information is becoming easily accessible on the Internet, whether it's medical information, travel information, or just plain chat rooms where people are interested in getting together and talking about a topic that they care about.

If we look at schools, we're going to have to play the primary role in getting this technology out to kids. Some of the statistics give us hope that we can really fulfill this mission: 90 percent of schools have some type of Internet access. Now, what that means varies quite widely. In some cases, that means a single computer—if you had to wait in line, you'd get very impatient for an individual student to actually have a chance to go out there, and really browse the Internet. So that figure, in some ways, overstates where we are.

Our goal should be that this Internet access should not just be in a lab somewhere, but it should be literally in every classroom. It should be part of the curriculum, and getting teachers enthused about bringing this in as a new tool. After all, every student starts out with amazing curiosity. They want to explore subjects, they want to find kids who have similar interests. And the Internet is fantastic for letting people go out and explore things on their own. And if it's done properly, you can bring back to the classroom the things that you found that were very interesting, and share those with all of the other kids.

Now, the number of Internet connections for each student in the United States is today about 14 students per Internet connection. That's much better than a year ago where it was 20, but still very far away from making it something that everybody gets a chance to use at leisure. The majority of schools report that teachers are really using the Internet, they're at least going out there to find materials that they can present in the classroom as well as involving in the kids in using the Internet. But the vision of what this should be is far different than we have right now. We talk about a "connected learning community" where the parents are going online and seeing what's being assigned. They're helping to research a topic, working together with their kids. And the curriculum itself has been redesigned to take full advantage of this.

And who are the kids that are going to have the full impact of this? Certainly the kids being born today, from 1994 on, they're a new generation, and nobody has really labeled this generation, so I would propose today that we think about calling this "Generation I." Of course, "I" for Internet. You know, these are kids who will always wonder why we talk about having records. To them, music will just be something you can get on your computer, and organized exactly the way you want and carry around with you however you want. To them, the idea that all the rich information should be easy to search and find, and that you should be able to find other kids in another country and speak to them about what their thinking is about that topic. They'll simply take that for granted. They'll think of buying as something where you can go out and get the best prices, or get the product reviews across the Internet. And so, they will think about the Internet in a far more profound way than most of us who grew up without it being an ever-present tool. And, in some ways, this is very, very exciting. These kids will be agents of change as they move out into their jobs. These kids include my own children. I've got a three-year-old and a four-month-old who are definitely going to be leading members of Generation I, and they have their high-speed Internet connection from the very beginning.

So, what will this lifestyle be like? Well, a lot of it will be saying that when you pull information together, you don't have to worry about writing it down on paper. You'll be able to go to the Internet and submit your homework that way. You'll be able to read books with very incredible screens. One of the things that is still ahead of us, but is definitely going to happen in the next three years, is to have flat panel screens that you can hold in your hands, just like the tablet, so it's comfortable to sit and read for long periods of time. That tablet display will have a resolution that makes it as comfortable as reading off of paper. I'm not saying that this will eliminate books, but it will give us a new flexibility to be able to call up material that otherwise wouldn't be easy to get to. And you can take textbooks and customize them for your class, take the portions that make sense from many different sources, and by bringing it together that way, the kids can browse it electronically. They can comment on parts of the text, send back something with a voice annotation or a handwriting annotation, whether they're confused about something they're reading or they want to make the comment on it.

That whole process of collaborating, letting kids show their ideas, will be very different than it's been—where we have to work strictly out of the textbooks that are often out of date, and not really tailored to that particular child's interest. Kids will all have a little smart card, so whatever PC or tablet they see, they just will run their smart card through the reader, and it will immediately bring up the things that they care about. Their electronic mail, their schedule, and they'll have access to that information wherever they go.

These kids won't think about the phone and the PC as being two different worlds. Whenever you're using the PC and you go to a Web site, you'll be able to click and talk to people, and likewise the phone that you carry around more and more will have a pretty good screen on it. And so, calling up things about the weather or new messages, all of that will be available from the phone as well as the PC. Likewise, the TV will let you connect up, not just playing great games, or getting any video you want, but also navigating the world of information. So, we'll have one set of standards around the Internet, and all of these devices connecting up to that common network.

So, it will be a world where everything is online, and that's simply taken for granted. And these kids will, in a creative way, build the Web sites that will make the Web sites we have today look like really nothing, sort of in the same way that you look at the early TV shows, early radio shows, and realize that the medium was not being fully exploited, there was so much more that could be done by people who really grew up with it and thought about it as central to their life.

Having all these devices makes it a lifestyle activity. You won't be surprised when you look at your small screen and say, okay, what's the traffic looks like, or what are my friends up to. That will just be something you expect to do all the time. All the material that's in the library today is slowly but surely being digitized. All the new books, the periodicals, and even the books from the past that are hard to get when they're in paper form. In fact, a little later we'll see a great example of how digital access is letting people see the history and get back to their roots in a way that wouldn't have been possible without digital technology. So, the Internet, the power in the microprocessor, the miracle of great software, and other advances like the flat screen displays, will make this far more natural to use. The interface will include speech recognition. You won't have to type everything that you're interested in, you'll simply be able to talk to the device and ask it to help you find the information.

So, this will really be the most incredible tool that's ever been created. The way that we get the most out of it is, we connect everything together. We have all the material that museums can put online, and have accessible for kids. We have people in the community, we have parents at home, and then we have the schools themselves all sharing across the Internet. So, the first time teachers will find that if they're teaching a subject in a particularly creative way, they can put up the material they're using and the approach they've taken onto the Internet, have other teachers find out, perhaps add things into it, and share it back to the original creator, and everyone else. In fact, I think there will be a lot of great awards that are given to teachers who go to the effort to take their good ideas, put them out on the Internet, and make them available to everyone else. So, whatever subject it is, whatever level it is, you'll be able to go out there and find neat, exciting ideas that really draw the kids in, that use examples that they can relate to by using the breadth of material that the richness of the Internet provides.

When I keep saying Internet, I don't just mean text pages, or even pages with just pictures. The Internet that we're talking about in the years ahead is one where audio and video are a full part of the experience. And so, if you want to have, say, an interactive experiment where the kid can play around with some of the different parameters, you can have rich software that can create a video experience showing you exactly what would happen when you change the different variables. So, if it's playing around with the physics equation, or the design of something, right there on the screen, you'll be able to get a lot of the feel of how the different inputs control the thing. And so you'll want to pursue that and go with your full curiosity to understand exactly how those things work. So the boundaries won't be the same as they've been today. And this connected learning community, the idea of everybody contributing, will be commonplace.

So what are the key things we need to do here? We need to get great content out there. We need to have rewards for everybody who is putting up that content. We need ways of classifying it and linking it together, so that it's easy for people to find something that they might want to be interested in. We need to get teachers involved, so that the design of learning is built around this. We need to make sure that it's not just a small percentage of the kids who've got access. We don't want to have a divide here, where the kids who have the Internet at home are able to go and do wonderful things, and the kids who don't have that access in their home don't have a way to have the equivalent experience. We want to make sure that we're avoiding material online that is damaging, so the idea of how you control that, how you train kids to use this in a responsible way—that's very, very important.

In terms of content, the progress here is pretty fantastic. One of the things that Microsoft got involved in very early on is the idea of taking the encyclopedia and creating a digital version. And so we created over five years ago what we call Encarta. And that was delivered on a CD, and included not just the text and pictures, but also audio and video. In some ways the encyclopedia is a great example of how digital information can be more accessible. Now, I remember when I was a kid I had a copy of the *World Book,* and I thought, well, how am I supposed to read this thing? Well, I read it alphabetically. But, it's kind of strange, because you're reading about the 1600s, then the 1800s, then the 1900s, and it's sort of hard to get a feel for the subject when that's the only way that the information is organized. And when information is changed, you get the year book every year and you paste in the labels, but you really haven't revised all the things that should be changed there.

Well, moving this into digital form means that you can navigate the subjects in a far more natural way. Tell me all the articles about the kings in England. Give me all the articles about great scientists. And so it's far more natural to pursue your curiosity and go through the material that way. You can have timelines, music, all the things that paper form doesn't provide. Another key point here, and one that shouldn't be missed, is that it can be very inexpensive. Today, for $40 or $50, these electronic encyclopedias provide far more information than even the print version that was very difficult for a lot of households to buy, because just the printing costs and everything made those cost $300 or $400. So the results are quite dramatic here. This is the first paper document where the electronic form is far more popular than the paper form....

I've said that we're going to have to put a lot of investment into thinking about how to teach this Generation I. You know, how does technology fit in? Technology by itself is not the answer. The answer is teachers, great teachers, who are using technology in the best way. And, there's a lot of investment to be made in these teachers. Really helping them to feel prepared for the modern classroom. It's got to be intimidating when you've got kids who, in some ways, are ahead of you in using this tool. You have no idea how you're going to control their usage, and you have a curriculum that you need to teach that really hasn't been adapted to fit the Internet and what can be done there. And so, it was interesting in a recent survey, only 20 percent of teachers said that they really feel prepared to bring in the technology in the right way. That's quite a stark contrast to the fact that, yes, we are creating the connections, and that's going to happen, but we haven't made the investment in the teachers to really bring them along and get them to drive this forward. And that's the only way it really can come together.

So, I think there is a clear call to action here. How do we make sure that the education curriculum is changed, how do we make sure that as teachers refresh their skills, they're really brought into this? How do we take those textbook budgets and really think not just about what's on paper, but also about what can be done on the Internet, and how those two things relate to each other?

So, there's a need for some massive training to be done, and this is a case where government at all levels, corporations, and philanthropists really need to come together to have this take place.

The kids today are anxious to have this opportunity. And so, the sooner we can get all the teachers to be enthusiastic about it, the better. There are many companies jumping in on this. We've done a lot of things ourselves with training labs. We have our Web site that we connect people up to training opportunities, and through our work, including the material we've created, over a million teachers have been trained. Now, compared to the need that's only getting part way there.

One of the programs that is most exciting that we've done is called "anywhere, anytime learning." And that's where you see that the best thing to do for a student is to actually give them their own computer. When they have their own computer, they have that sense of ownership, they don't have to stand in line to use it, they can go home at night, if there's something they're confused about they get as much time as they want, they can sit with their friends and talk about it. The teacher can know that every kid in the classroom has this tool. That's where you get the greatest impact. And we call that anywhere, anytime learning, because this is a program based on getting portable computers to all the kids, and then connecting up the network in the classrooms so they can print, and display their information. There are 500 schools around the world who've adopted this idea, and it's something that the results have really been quite fantastic....

Getting the prices of the machines down, so you can have them at home, coming up with special financing options for things like laptops, that's very important. The schools themselves, whether it's special levies, or allocation of resources towards technology, clearly that's a very central role. The libraries are another place that can be part of this. That's one area where the foundation that I created has helped to make sure that over the next several years every library in the United States, all 16,000, will have a state of the art PC with an Internet connection. So kids who can reach the library can get in and take advantage of that. And the usage of that has been quite phenomenal.

We should also reach out to community centers, any clubs, any place where the kids go we should make sure that the technology is there. Now there is special work that needs to be done to make sure that the kids are using this tool in a constructive fashion, and that they understand some of the things they ought to know and be careful about. We've worked together with Boys and Girls Club to come up with what we call the Stay Safe Online program, it's the kind of things that teachers, or a community center, or parents can go through with children who are using this tool, and really give them guidelines about how it should be used properly. And so that's, we think, an important element of how this can move forward.

There's no doubt in my mind that we've got a fantastic opportunity here. The people at Microsoft who work on creating the software that's part of it, part of the reason they love their job is they know that these tools will be used in education in some exciting ways. We're really just at the very beginning of this, but I can say with great confidence that the Internet is going to change education as fundamentally as it changed when we had printed books. And that's something that it's going to be very exciting to be a part of.

Source: Gates, Bill. Remarks at New York Institute of Technology, October 28, 1999. Available online at http://www.microsoft.com/billgates/speeches/10-28GenI.asp.

A Newspaper Columnist Laments the Dangers of the Internet

Despite the obvious benefits of the Internet, the vast computer network also exposes users to a variety of risks. For example, hackers can use high-speed connections to gain access to other people's home computers and business networks in order to steal information or use the systems for their own purposes. Programs known as adware can slow down computers by placing an endless series of "pop-up" advertisements on the screen. Other programs known as spyware can record the Web sites a user visits and target advertising directly toward that person's interests.

Perhaps the most frightening of the Internet dangers are the malicious programs known as viruses. Viruses may be accidentally downloaded simultaneously with useful programs, or sent via e-mail attachments. Once they infect a system, they can destroy data, steal personal information, corrupt system files, and render a computer worthless. In the following column for USA Today, *Kevin Maney recalls his struggles to rid his home computer of an Internet virus.*

Now I'm really mad. A virus killed my family's computer.

Not just a little cough-cough I'm clogged with spyware and slowing down kind of thing. We're talking a senseless, untimely death.

I'm past denial. Deep into anger.

It was probably the Sasser virus, according to my new best friends on the Microsoft help desk. Sasser allegedly was released by a middle-class German teenager named Sven Jaschan earlier this year. He was charged with sabotage last week by German police.

If Jaschan did it, jail would be the safest place for him, because I would be just one of a few million people who would like to do him harm.

Anger about this stuff is spreading as fast as the viruses. At our end-of-summer block party, I mentioned to a group of neighbors that a virus had crashed our PC. Instantly, every one of them launched into stories about unstoppable blitzes of adware (which throws pop-up ads on your screen, or worse) and spyware (which can find stuff on your PC and send it somewhere) and computers brought down by viruses.

One dad—a former military guy who no doubt has handled weapons—vowed that if he caught someone who released a virus, he'd kill the person

---

Maney, Kevin. "Your Computer May Not Be as Protected as You Think It Is," September 15, 2004. *USA Today.* Copyright © 2004. Reprinted with permission.

and proudly mount the body on the mailbox in front of his house for all to see. The rest of us applauded the idea, though we concurred that the home-owners association probably wouldn't allow it.

The same conversations could happen in any neighborhood. The viruses and adware are particularly whacking home and small-business users, who don't have the heavy-duty protection corporations install. Millions of home computers have been hit.

My computer was only 18 months old. I wasn't totally naive. My broad-band Internet came into a router, which provided something of a firewall—a barrier to keep the riff-raff out. I had one anti-virus program and one anti-spyware program running.

But about six weeks ago, the runaway adware started. No telling why. Someone in my house could've clicked on the wrong thing. But trying to knock the ads down was like playing Whac-A-Mole.

I ran software to clean it up. I switched from Microsoft Explorer Web browser to Mozilla's Firefox, since the bad guys mostly pick on Explorer. I almost got the situation under control.

And then one morning as the PC started to boot, a box popped up saying something about a "remote procedure call." It said Windows had to restart. So Windows rebooted, came to that same point, showed the same "remote procedure call" box, and again restarted. My PC was doomed to a continuous loop of never turning off but never starting—a computer purgatory. This was the virus at work.

Now what? The last thing I wanted to do was call a help line and talk to someone in the Philippines. Besides, what help line do you call? Microsoft? The PC maker? Dr. Phil?

Instead, I asked techie friends for advice. This is how I learned things about Windows that I would rather not have to know—the tech equivalent of learning how your bowels function.

Press F8 as Windows is booting, my friends told me. Try to launch in "safe mode"—who knew there was a safe mode?—and run anti-virus software from a disk. Maybe that will clean it out.

For this, I figured I'd buy some new anti-virus software. I went to the computer store. The anti-virus/anti-spam/firewall aisle was half empty. It looked like the six-shooter aisle at the Dodge City general store the day after an outlaw gang rode into town. Obviously another sign of the spreading Internet security panic.

186

Rich Kilmer, a tech entrepreneur who lives near me, pointed out the Web site www.windowsreinstall.com. It shows every screen you see when doing these crazy Windows maneuvers. Tremendously helpful.

Anyway, I tried safe mode, which wouldn't work. It could've been operator error—I don't know. But my PC got worse. The hard drive froze solid as a caveman in an avalanche.

That's when I gave up and called Microsoft.

Two very smart and patient technicians spent three hours on the phone with me. After the first few minutes analyzing the situation, one of them said, "Ohhhh," in the way that doctors say "Ohhhh" when the blood test shows your cholesterol number has four digits. "That's bad," he said.

We installed a second copy of Windows XP Home on the same computer, copied most of my personal files—photos, documents, music—that I wanted to save, and concluded that the PC as it existed was a goner. The virus had corrupted the operating system and probably did so much damage, in so many places, it would be impossible to repair the existing software.

The hard drive would have to be wiped clean or replaced, a new copy of Windows XP installed, and all my other software and files reinstalled. It's essentially the same as starting from scratch with a new PC.

I have since learned that I was more naive than I thought. In-the-know tech people these days constantly run three or four software programs such as Spybot and Adaware to keep the ads and spyware and other annoying stuff to a minimum. On top of that, they run firewall software on their PCs and don't just rely on a router. They run at least one anti-virus program and make sure they get the automatic updates, which come in over the Internet and add protection against newly discovered viruses.

I found out the hard way that it's a new world out there on the Internet. It feels like living in Mayberry RFD one minute and Blade Runner the next. We had been able to leave the doors unlocked, but suddenly we find ourselves installing bars on the windows and multiple alarm systems.

It's sick. And I'm still ticked off.

Source: Maney, Kevin. "Your Computer May Not Be as Protected as You Think It Is." *USA Today*, September 15, 2004, p.B3.

SOURCES FOR FURTHER STUDY

Gralla, Preston. *How the Internet Works.* 7th ed. Indianapolis, IN: Que, 2004. This informative text provides an overview of the technical aspects of the Internet's operation, using language and format accessible to students. It includes details about the inner workings of routers, wireless networks, search engines, instant messaging, viruses, spyware, and many other aspects of the online experience.

Hafner, Katie, and Matthew Lyon. *Where Wizards Stay Up Late: The Origins of the Internet.* New York: Simon and Schuster, 1998. A fascinating account of the early development of the Internet, beginning with the conception of the ARPANET in the 1960s and ending with the decommissioning of this first computer network in 1990.

Internet Society. "All About the Internet." http://www.isoc.org/internet. The online home of one of the Internet's governing organizations, this site includes a wealth of information about the development and growth of the network, as well as links to histories, biographies, and important documents.

National Museum of American History. "Birth of the Internet." http://smithsonian.yahoo.com/birthoftheinternet.html. Compiled by the Smithsonian Institution and Yahoo!, this site offers information on important people, companies, and events in the history of the Internet and World Wide Web.

Richards, Sally. *FutureNet: The Past, Present, and Future of the Internet as Told by Its Creators and Visionaries.* New York: John Wiley and Sons, 2002. Such famous Internet pioneers as Vint Cerf and Leonard Kleinrock reminisce about the challenges of bringing the Internet to life and speculate about the possible directions the technology might take in the future.

Segaller, Stephen. *Nerds 2.0.1: A Brief History of the Internet.* New York: TV Books, 1998. As the title implies, this book focuses on the technological pioneers who contributed to the development, growth, and commercialization of computer networking. It provides an entertaining yet informative account of the history of the Internet through the personal stories of its creators.

BIBLIOGRAPHY

Books and Periodicals

Abbate, Janet. *Inventing the Internet.* Cambridge, MA: MIT Press, 1999.

Abram, Stephen. "Twenty Reasons to Love IM." *Information Outlook,* October 2004.

"The Abridged History of the Internet." *Internet Magazine,* January 2004.

Angel, Karen. *Inside Yahoo! Reinvention and the Road Ahead.* New York: John Wiley, 2002.

Berners-Lee, Tim, with Mark Fischetti. *Weaving the Web: The Original Design and Ultimate Destiny of the World Wide Web.* New York: HarperCollins, 1999.

Brody, Herb. "Net Cerfing." *Technology Review,* May-June 1998.

Ceruzzi, Paul E. *A History of Modern Computing.* 2nd ed. Cambridge, MA: MIT Press, 2003.

Conner-Sax, Kiersten, and Ed Krol. *The Whole Internet: The Next Generation.* Sebastapol, CA: O'Reilly and Associates, 1999.

Conrades, George. "The Future of the Internet: Predicting the Unpredictable." *Vital Speeches of the Day,* April 1, 1998.

Cothran, Helen, ed. *The Internet: Opposing Viewpoints.* San Diego, CA: Greenhaven Press, 2002.

Dolliver, Mark. "The Digital Divide Just Isn't What It Used to Be: 'Quality of Access.'" *Adweek,* September 27, 2004.

"The Dot-Com Bubble Bursts." *New York Times,* December 24, 2000.

Egendorf, Laura K., ed. *The Information Revolution: Opposing Viewpoints.* San Diego, CA: Greenhaven Press, 2004.

Ferren, Bran. "The Future of the Internet." *Discover,* November 2000.

Gates, Bill. *The Road Ahead.* New York: Viking, 1995.

Gonsalves, Antone. "Internet Posts Fastest Growth in Political Spending." *Internet Week,* August 19, 2004.

Graham, Ian. *The Internet: The Impact on Our Lives.* Austin, TX: Raintree Steck-Vaughn, 2001.

Gralla, Preston. *How the Internet Works.* 7th ed. Indianapolis, IN: Que, 2004.

Grossman, Lev. "It's All Free!" *Time Almanac,* 2004.

Hafner, Katie, and Matthew Lyon. *Where Wizards Stay Up Late: The Origins of the Internet.* New York: Simon and Schuster, 1998.

Henderson, Harry. *History Makers: Pioneers of the Internet.* San Diego: Lucent Books, 2002.

Holcombe, Carl D. "Internet's Future Is Faster, More Accessible, Versatile." *Arkansas Business,* July 19, 2004.

"Inside Yahoo!" *Business Week,* May 21, 2001.

Klein, Alec. *Stealing Time: Steve Case, Jerry Levin, and the Collapse of AOL Time Warner.* New York: Simon and Schuster, 2003.

Leonard, Andrew. "We've Got Mail—Always: It Saves Time and Wastes It, Makes Life Simpler and More Complicated, Brings Us Together and Pushes Us Apart." *Newsweek,* September 20, 1999.

Leone, Richard C., and Greg Anrig, Jr. *The War on Our Freedoms: Civil Liberties in an Age of Terrorism.* Washington, DC: Public Affairs, 2003.

Levy, Steven, Brad Stone, and Peter Suciu. "All Eyes on Google." *Newsweek,* March 29, 2004.

Lewis, Michael. *Next: The Future Just Happened.* New York: W.W. Norton, 2001.

Lohr, Steve. "The Economy Transformed, Bit by Bit." *New York Times,* December 20, 1999.

Loughran, Donna. *Technology and You: Internet History.* Austin, TX: Steck-Vaughn, 2003.

Maney, Kevin. "Next Big Thing: The Web as Your Servant." *USA Today,* October 1, 2004.

McHugh, Joseph. "Web Warrior." *Forbes,* January 11, 1999.

Moritz, Gwen. "How Did We Live?" *Arkansas Business,* July 19, 2004.

Motavalli, John. *Bamboozled at the Revolution: How Big Media Lost Billions in the Battle for the Internet.* New York: Viking Penguin, 2002.

Mullaney, Timothy J. "The E-Biz Surprise: It Wasn't All Hype." *Business Week,* May 12, 2003.

Munk, Nina. "Steve Case's Last Stand." *Vanity Fair,* January 2003.

Munro, Neil. "When the Dot-Com Bubble Burst." *National Journal,* February 10, 2001.

Naughton, John. *A Brief History of the Future: Origins of the Internet.* London: Orion, 2000.

Notess, Greg R. "A Decade on the Net." *Online,* March-April 2003.

Randall, Neil. *The Soul of the Internet: Net Gods, Netizens, and the Wiring of the World.* New York: International Thompson Computer Press, 1997.

Rebello, Kathy. "Inside Microsoft: The Untold Story of How the Internet Forced Bill Gates to Change Course." *Business Week,* July 15, 1996.

Reid, Robert H. *Architects of the Web: 1,000 Days that Built the Future of Business.* New York: John Wiley and Sons, 1997.

Richards, Sally. *FutureNet: The Past, Present, and Future of the Internet as Told by Its Creators and Visionaries.* New York: John Wiley and Sons, 2002.

Segaller, Stephen. *Nerds 2.0.1: A Brief History of the Internet.* New York: TV Books, 1998.

Sherman, Josepha. *The History of the Internet.* New York: Franklin Watts, 2003.

Stevens, Chris. "Welcome to the House of the Future." *Internet Magazine,* January 2004.

Stone, Brad. "New Valley Rules." *Newsweek,* March 12, 2001.

Swisher, Kara. *AOL.com: How Steve Case Beat Bill Gates, Nailed the Netheads, and Made Millions in the War for the Web.* New York: Crown, 1998.

Swisher, Kara. *There Must Be a Pony in Here Somewhere: The AOL Time Warner Debacle and the Quest for a Digital Future.* New York: Crown, 2003.

"Through a Glass Darkly." *The Economist,* January 25, 2003.

U.S. Department of Commerce. *A Nation Online: How Americans Are Expanding Their Use of the Internet.* Washington, DC: February 2002.

Weinberger, David. *Small Pieces Loosely Joined: A Unified Theory of the Web.* Cambridge, MA: Perseus, 2002.

Wilder, Clinton. "It's Time to Get Real—The Glory Days of the Tech Boom Are Over. Have We Learned Any Lessons?" *Information Week,* June 4, 2001.

Online

Cerf, Vinton. "A Brief History of the Internet and Related Networks." Internet Society, http://www.isoc.org/internet/history/cerf.shtml.

Charles Babbage Institute, Center for the History of Information Technology, University of Minnesota. "Oral History Collection." http://www.cbi.umn.edu/oh.

Glasner, Joanna. "Conversation with Marc Andreessen." *Wired.com,* February 14, 2003. Available online at http://www.wired.com/news/business/0,1367,57661,00.html.

"Google Corporate Information, Google History." *Google.com,* undated. Available online at www.google.com/corporate/history.html.

Internet Society. "All About the Internet." http://www.isoc.org/internet.

Kharif, Olga. "The Net: Now, Folks Can't Live without It." *Business Week Online,* June 10, 2003. http:www.businessweek.com/technology/content/jun2003/tc20030610_1865_tc104.htm.

Leiner, Barry, et al. "A Brief History of the Internet." Internet Society, http://www.isoc.org/internet/history/brief.shtml.

Lerner, Michael. "Learn the Net." http://www.learnthenet.com.

National Museum of American History. "Birth of the Internet." http://smithsonian.yahoo.com/birthoftheinternet.html.

Pew Internet and American Life Project. http://www.pewinternet.org.

Robinson, Teri. "Lasting Benefits of the Dot-Com Bubble." *E-Commerce Times,* Oct. 21, 2004. http://www.ecommercetimes.com/story/18570.html.

Stewart, William. "The Living Internet." http://livinginternet.com.

World Wide Web Consortium. http://www.w3.org.

Video

Nerds 2.0.1: A Brief History of the Internet (VHS). PBS Home Video, 1998.

PHOTO CREDITS

INDEX